RURAL CRIMINOLOGY

Rural crime is a fast growing area of interest among scholars in criminology. From studies of agricultural crime in Australia, to violence against women in Appalachia America, to poaching in Uganda, to land theft in Brazil – the criminology community has come to recognize that crime manifests itself in rural localities in ways that both conform to and challenge conventional theory and research. For the first time, *Rural Criminology* brings together contemporary research and conceptual considerations to synthesize rural crime studies from a critical perspective.

This book dispels four rural crime myths, challenging conventional criminological theories about crime in general. It also examines both the historical development of rural crime scholarship and recent research and conceptual developments. The third chapter recreates the critical in the rural criminology literature through discussions of three important topics: community characteristics and rural crime; drug use, production, and trafficking in the rural context; and agricultural crime.

Never before has rural crime been examined comprehensively, using any kind of theoretical approach, whether critical or otherwise. *Rural Criminology* does both, pulling together in one short volume the diverse array of empirical research under the theoretical umbrella of a critical perspective. This book will be of interest to those studying or researching in the fields of rural crime, critical criminology, and sociology.

Joseph F. Donnermeyer is a Professor of Rural Sociology in the School of Environment and Natural Resources at The Ohio State University. Dr. Donnermeyer is an internationally known expert on rural crime and is the editor of the *International Journal of Rural Criminology*. He is the author/co-author of over 100 peer reviewed journal articles, book chapters, and books on issues related to rural crime and rural societies. Dr. Donnermeyer was the winner of The Ohio State University Alumni Association Award for Distinguished Teaching in 2004, and served as chair of the OSU Academy of Teaching from 2005–2010.

Walter S. DeKeseredy is Anna Deane Carlson Endowed Chair of Social Sciences at West Virginia University. He has published 18 books and over 160 scientific journal articles and book chapters on violence against women and other social problems. In 2008, the Institute on Violence, Abuse and Trauma gave him the Linda Saltzman Memorial Intimate Partner Violence Researcher Award. He also jointly received the 2004 Distinguished Scholar Award from the American Society of Criminology's (ASC) Division on Women and Crime and the 2007 inaugural UOIT Research Excellence Award. In 1995, he received the Critical Criminologist of the Year Award from the ASC's Division on Critical Criminology (DCC) and in 2008 the DCC gave him the Lifetime Achievement Award.

New Directions in Critical Criminology

Edited by Walter S. DeKeseredy

WEST VIRGINIA UNIVERSITY

This series presents new cutting-edge critical criminological empirical, theoretical, and policy work on a broad range of social problems, including drug policy, rural crime and social control, policing and the media, ecocide, intersectionality, and the gendered nature of crime. It aims to highlight the most up-to-date authoritative essays written by new and established scholars in the field. Rather than offering a survey of the literature, each book takes a strong position on topics of major concern to those interested in seeking new ways of thinking critically about crime.

1. Contemporary Drug Policy

Henry H. Brownstein

2. The Treadmill of Crime

Political economy and green criminology
Paul B. Stretesky, Michael A. Long and Michael J. Lynch

3. Rural Criminology

Joseph F. Donnermeyer and Walter S. DeKeseredy

RURAL CRIMINOLOGY

*Joseph F. Donnermeyer and
Walter S. DeKeseredy*

Routledge
Taylor & Francis Group

LONDON AND NEW YORK

First published 2014
by Routledge
2 Park Square, Milton Park, Abingdon, Oxon OX14 4RN

and by Routledge
711 Third Avenue, New York, NY 10017

Routledge is an imprint of the Taylor & Francis Group, an informa business

British Library Cataloguing in Publication Data
A catalogue record for this book is available from the British
Library

Library of Congress Cataloging-in-Publication Data
DeKeseredy, Walter S.
Rural criminology / Joseph F. Donnermeyer and Walter S.
DeKeseredy.
    pages cm. – (New directions in critical criminology)
    1. Rural crimes. 2. Criminology. I. Donnermeyer, Joseph
F. II. Title.
    HV6791.D45 2014
    364.9173'4–dc23

                                          2013011530

ISBN: 978-0-415-63435-9 (hbk)
ISBN: 978-0-415-63438-0 (pbk)
ISBN: 978-0-203-09451-8 (ebk)

Typeset in Bembo and Stone Sans
by Wearset Ltd, Boldon, Tyne and Wear

CONTENTS

FIGURES

BOXES

PREFACE

Described in greater detail in Chapter 2, the roots of this book were sown nearly 10 years ago at Morretti's Italian restaurant in Upper Arlington, Ohio. It was there that we first met and our instant intellectual partnership eventually culminated in this project and many other scholarly products. We have learned much from each other over the past 10 years, but that there is a need for a comprehensive, critical criminological book on rural crime and social control is something that no one had to teach us. This is not to say that good books on rural crime have not been published in the past. Indeed, there are a few, and some of them are decidedly critical monographs. Still, those that deviate from mainstream or orthodox thinking about violations of legal and social norms and societal reactions to these transgressions did not review as wide a range of progressive empirical, theoretical, and political offerings as we have done here. This is not, by any means, a criticism of our colleagues' fine work because our book, in the words of the late sociologist Robert K. Merton, stands on the shoulders of these giants. Note, too, that there was no way near as much critical criminological scholarly work available on the topics we address as there is today. As well, the bulk of rural criminological work has only been published over the past two decades, and we hope this monograph accelerates the field's progress.

Rural Criminology has several major objectives, one of which is to review our international colleagues' scholarly efforts to enhance a critical or progressive understanding of crime, law, and social control in rural places. One thing all of our peers have in common is that they challenge popular myths about rural crime and this is the main goal of Chapter 1.

Additionally, the realities of rural crime are described there and many readers will be surprised to discover that the rates of certain crimes are higher in rural communities than they are in suburban and urban areas. As well, we hope that our extensive list of references on rural crime, which we believe to be the first extensive compilation since the last edition of the Weisheit, Falcone, and Wells' book in 2006, will encourage other scholars to focus their research and theorizing on the rural.

In Chapter 2, we trace the origins of rural critical criminology and pay homage to the path-breaking sociologist/criminologist William (Bill) Chambliss. Much respect is also given to feminist rural scholarly efforts that started in the early 1990s because they, too, helped pave the way for a critical *Rural Criminology*.

Chapter 3 briefly reviews the most salient empirical work done by an international cadre of rural criminologists and, like Chapter 2, encourages us to keep moving forward and to focus on new areas of social scientific inquiry. Since much of the rural work is not critical in focus, we used Chapter 3 to reinterpret scholarship on community and rural crime, rural drug use, production and trafficking, and agricultural crime in a more critical form. We accomplish this task by adopting the square of crime to help organize concepts and literature, but we eschew claiming any high ground on the use of this left realist concept as superior to other critical criminological perspectives. Simply, our goal is to sharpen the conceptual focus of a literature that heretofore has been mostly descriptive and theory-less.

What is to be done about crime, law, and social control in rural places? In Chapter 4, we begin by acknowledging the diversity of rural topics we did not review in Chapter 3, and emphasize that since nearly half of the world is rural, we sincerely hope more criminology scholars begin to see the relevance of rural criminology to the general discipline of criminology and to its advancement. The policy and practice discussed in Chapter 4 are heavily informed by work done previously by our progressive peers over the past 30 years, and we offer what we strongly believe to be effective answers to this question. Race, class, and gender issues are treated as being equally important, but there is an ample amount of pessimism scattered throughout our suggestions. For critical criminologists, this shouldn't be surprising and we assume that many, if not most of them, would concur with what Elliott Currie (2013) recently observed:

> I have a lot of friends who have told me lately that they no longer read newspapers. This isn't because they get their news on the Internet now, but because they can't stand to read news at all because the news is so grim. I haven't gone that far, but I am sympathetic. It's undeniable that reading the paper today is a fairly grueling experience, because the news seems to be full of almost nothing but accounts of the various crises that afflict much of the planet. In particular, the global economic order most of us live under – so–called "free-market" capitalism – seems to lurch from crisis to crisis and indeed often seems to be in a state of perpetual emergency.
>
> *(p. 3)*

To be sure, if you are left-wing, there is not much to be optimistic about in this current neo-liberal era characterized by rabid corporate greed, numerous assaults on Indigenous sovereignty and the environment, growing international racism and xenophobia disguised as "national security measures," and widespread sexism and homophobia. An even longer list of hurtful symptoms of structured social inequality that critical criminologists study could be provided here. Even so, the struggle for crime, justice, and social democracy must continue and critical rural criminologists and other types of progressive thinkers and activists must support each other as we continue to be under siege and face even more turbulent times.

ACKNOWLEDGMENTS

This book is a product of many discussions and other types of scholarly exchanges with our kind, innovative, and energetic peers. Nonetheless, the most important impetus was Thomas (Tom) Sutton, our good friend and colleague at Routledge. Many social scientists have good or great ideas, yet never put them on paper. Tom wouldn't let us get away with that and strongly encouraged us at the 2011 American Society of Criminology conference in Washington, DC, to draft a proposal. We are deeply grateful that he motivated us to do so because not only did we write this book, but we were also prompted to review materials that would not have otherwise read and incorporated into our presentation and critical analysis of rural criminology scholarship. Special thanks go to another great person at Routledge – Nicola Hartley. She kept us on schedule and went beyond the call of duty in ways too numerous to mention here.

Most of this book was written during a time of much pain and sorrow for Walter DeKeseredy. In 2012, he lost three loving family members in a five-month time period, including his mother, and he faced other grueling types of life-events stress. Nonetheless, he persevered and could not have overcome these challenges without the ongoing friendship and emotional support of many of the great people acknowledged below. Joseph Donnermeyer, too, had "crosses to bear," including the loss of his mother-in-law (Mary Ona Bacon) in 2012.

Joe and Walt's friends and colleagues were "rock solid" in support of their efforts to develop a sophisticated social scientific corpus of knowledge about rural crime, law, and social control. We have learned much from them over the years and wish to recognize them here – Etiony Alderando, Rowland Atkinson, Bernie Auchter, Karen Bachar, Gregg Barak, Elaine Barclay, Raquel Kennedy Bergen, Helene Berman, David Bird, Henry Brownstein, Susan Caringella, Kerry Carrington, Liqun Cao, Meda Chesney-Lind, Ann Coker, Kimberly J. Cook, Wesley Crichlow, Francis T. Cullen, Elliott Currie, Kathleen Daly, Molly Dragiewicz, Ruth Edwards, Desmond Ellis, Jeff Ferrell, Bonnie Fisher, Alberto Godenzi, Judith Grant, Steve Hall, Domingo Herraiz, Ronald Hinch, Russell Hogg, Pat Jobes, David Kauzlarich, Marie Kaylen, Dorie Klein, Julian Lo, Michael J. Lynch, Brian D. MacLean, James W. Messerschmidt, Raymond J. Michalowski, Jody Miller, Susan L. Miller, Dragan Milovanovic, Louise Moyer, Heather Nancarrow, Ana Neves, the late G. Howard Phillips, Eugene Oetting, Patrik Olsson, Barbara Owen, Julia L. Perilla, Ruth Peterson, Lori Post, Mike Presdee, William Pridemore, Claire M. Renzetti, Robin Robinson, Jeffrey Ian Ross, Scott Scheer, Martin D. Schwartz, John Scott, Aysan Sev'er, Susan Sharp, the late Michael D. Smith, Cris Sullivan, Betsy Stanko, Kenneth D. Tunnell, Ralph Weisheit, Jeremy Wilson, Simon Winlow, and Jock Young. Because many of these people disagree with one another, we assume full responsibility for the material presented in this book.

Rural Criminology would not have been completed without the ongoing support of various Donnermeyer and DeKeseredy family members. On Joe's side of the ledger is the love, hugs, support and criticisms of his wife, Diane. Joe's grandchildren – Dominic, Damian, and Skylar – were a constant source of delightful interruption from his work. By taking him out of his work, even when baby-sitting, Lego block projects and general play seemed like a conflict of time and energy with his need to meet writing deadlines, they helped him look at the thoughts and words in this book in a fresh way, once he was able to return to his office (generally after a nap). He also acknowledges his love for his grown-up children, Christopher and Melanie, and for their spouses (his grown up children-in-law), Jen Kevil and Michael Richards.

Pat (Walt's spouse) and Andrea (his daughter) DeKeseredy have seen him sweat through completion of over 18 book projects, and with each, Walter is grateful for their love and support. Walter's "fur children" Bennie, Captain, Drew, Mr. Higgins, Ola B. (named after feminist psychologist Ola Barnett), and Phoebe were additional sources of much support. Sadly, Drew and Ola B. died in the summer of 2012 and will, like Walter's mother, be forever missed. Animals are also family members and they constantly reminded Walter that critical criminologists need to think about the roles played by cats and dogs in the day-to-day struggle to eliminate all forms of inequality in all kinds of communities.

Joe is grateful for a supportive environment to strive toward excellence in both the scholarship of research and teaching provided by the School of Environment and Natural Resources, and of his Rural Sociology colleagues at The Ohio State University. Plus, he wishes to acknowledge the support of the Ohio Agricultural Research and Development Center, the research arm of the College of Food, Agricultural and Environmental Sciences. In addition to receiving funds to gather some of the data presented in this book from the U.S. Justice Department, Walter DeKeseredy obtained financial assistance from the College of Arts and Sciences and the Office of the Vice President of Research at Ohio University. Arguments and findings included in this book are our own, and do not represent the official position of the U.S. Department of Justice, The Ohio State University, or Ohio University.

This book includes material adapted from Walter S. DeKeseredy, "Review of Elliott Currie's *The Road to Whatever: Middle-Class Culture and the Crisis of Adolescence*," *Critical Criminology* (2007); Walter S. DeKeseredy, "Canadian Crime Control in the New Millennium: The Influence of Neo-Conservative U.S. Policies and Practices," *Police Practice and Research: An International Journal* (2009); Walter S. DeKeseredy, Shahid Alvi, Claire Renzetti, and Martin D. Schwartz, "Reducing Private Violence Against Women in Public Housing: Can Second Generation CPTED Make a Difference?" *CPTED Journal* (2004); Walter S. DeKeseredy and Joseph F. Donnermeyer, "Thinking Critically about Rural Crime: Toward the Development of a New Left Realist Perspective," in Simon Winlow and Rowland Atkinson (Eds.), *New Directions in Crime and Deviancy* (2013); Walter S. DeKeseredy, Joseph F. Donnermeyer, and Martin D. Schwartz, "Toward a Gendered Second Generation CPTED for Preventing Woman Abuse in Rural Communities," *The Security Journal* (2009); Walter S. DeKeseredy, Joseph F. Donnermeyer, Martin D. Schwartz, Kenneth D. Tunnell, and Mandy Hall, "Thinking Critically about Rural Gender Relations: Toward a Rural Masculinity Crisis/Male Peer Support Model of Separation/Divorce

Sexual Assault," *Critical Criminology* (2007); Walter S. DeKeseredy and Molly Dragiewicz, "Introduction," in Walter S. DeKeseredy and Molly Dragiewicz (Eds.), *Routledge International Handbook of Critical Criminology* (2012); Walter S. DeKeseredy, Desmond Ellis, and Shahid Alvi, *Deviance and Crime: Theory: Theory, Research and Policy* (2005); Walter S. DeKeseredy, Stephen L. Muzzatti, and Joseph F. Donnermeyer, "Mad Men in Bib Overalls: Media's Horrification and Pornification of Rural Culture," *Critical Criminology* (2013); Walter S. DeKeseredy, McKenzie Rogness, and Martin D. Schwartz, "Separation/Divorce Sexual Assault: The Current State of Social Scientific Knowledge," *Aggression and Violent Behavior* (2004); Walter S. DeKeseredy and Martin D. Schwartz, *Dangerous Exits: Escaping Abusive Relationships in Rural America* (2009); Walter S. DeKeseredy and Martin D. Schwartz, *Male Peer Support and Violence Against Women: The History and Verification of a Theory* (2014); Joseph F. Donnermeyer, "Rural Crime and Critical Criminology," in Walter S. DeKeseredy and Molly Dragiewicz (Eds.), *Routledge International Handbook of Critical Criminology* (2012); Joseph F. Donnermeyer, Pat Jobes, and Elaine Barclay, "Sociological Theory, Social Change, and Crime in Rural Communities" in A. Denis and D. Kalekin-Fishman (Eds.), *The ISA Handbook in Contemporary Sociology: Conflict, Competition, Cooperation* (2009); Joseph F. Donnermeyer and Walter S. DeKeseredy, "Toward a Rural Critical Criminology," *Southern Rural Sociology* (2008); and Joseph F. Donnermeyer, Walter S. DeKeseredy, and Molly Dragiewicz, "Policing Rural Canada and the United States," in Rob I. Mawby and Richard Yarwood (Eds.), *Rural Policing and Policing the Rural: A Constable Countryside?* (2011).

1

RURAL CRIME

Myths and realities

> Across the globe, rural communities and small towns are undergoing fundamental, and at times rapid, change. Within some rural areas of the U.S.A., the decline of the family farm and the housing development of the countryside race along. In addition, the Wal-Marting of rural America and the demise of locally owned and operated businesses alter the small-town landscape. Once-quaint hamlets are becoming vastly different places to those only a generation ago.
>
> *(Tunnell, 2006, p. 332)*

On any given evening, especially in North America, mainstream television stations and cable/satellite networks routinely broadcast fictional crime shows and films. Certainly, what West (1984, p. 3) stated nearly 30 years ago still holds true today: "Prime-time North American television is more than half filled with police dramas." Recent U.S. examples of such popular shows are *Blue Bloods*, *Hawaii Five-0*, and *Criminal Minds*. Although highly entertaining for thousands of viewers, these and other crime shows undoubtedly have some influence on numerous people's perceptions and opinions about crime and criminal justice system responses to it. In fact, for many people, fictional and nonfictional television shows, movies, and social media broadcasts or announcements are their major sources of information on crime and its control. For example, television viewing ranks as the third most time-consuming activity for U.S. citizens, and today, the amount of crime programming available on television is larger than ever (Surette, 2011). A key question, however, becomes, are all types of crime equally covered by the mass media? As you can answer for yourself: of course not. Violent and gang-related crimes receive the most attention. But in which geographic areas? The answer to this question is also obvious – big cities like New York and Los Angeles.

The academic criminological community provides superior information about crime in general, but most members of this rapidly growing international cohort of scholars are just as guilty as the mass media of focusing mainly on crimes in urban settings, despite strong evidence of high rates of certain crimes in rural places. Actually, rural crime has ranked among the least studied social problems in criminology (DeKeseredy, Donnermeyer, Schwartz, Tunnell, & Hall, 2007). As Donnermeyer, Jobes, and Barclay (2006) put it in their review of the rural crime literature:

> If rural crime was considered at all, it was a convenient "ideal type" contrasted with the criminogenic conditions assumed to exist exclusively in urban locations. Rural crime was rarely examined, either comparatively with urban crime or as a subject worthy of investigation in its own right.
>
> *(p. 199)*

This book, then, helps fill a major research gap by devoting much empirical, theoretical, and political attention to crimes and societal reactions to them in rural places. Of course, this is not the first social scientific volume on this topic. But, it is among the very few published so far to be driven by critical criminological ways of knowing and understanding. More specifically, consistent with our previous offerings (DeKeseredy & Donnermeyer, 2013; DeKeseredy et al., 2007; Donnermeyer, 2012; Donnermeyer & DeKeseredy, 2008), our main objective is to show the utility of critical criminology for the study of rural crime, and how a critical approach can give the scholarly consideration of rural crime a much greater significance, with many important implications that in turn can inform the general field of criminology and advance its theoretical development.

Definition of critical criminology[1]

It is painfully obvious, but worth stating again nonetheless: defining critical criminology is subject to much debate and there is no widely accepted precise formulation (DeKeseredy, 2011a; Stubbs, 2008). Hence, for the purpose of this book, critical criminology is viewed as a polyglot of concepts, theories, and interpretations about crime, deviance, and social control. Readers will be exposed to critical criminologies that have different origins, use multiple methods, and reflect diverse political beliefs. For instance, scattered throughout this book are reviews of rural work done by feminists, Marxists, left realists, cultural criminologists, and other types of critical criminologists.[2] Nonetheless, many versions of critical criminology can be summed up as perspectives that see crime as

> rooted in economic, social, and political inequalities, along with social class divisions, racism and hate, and other forms of segmented social organization, reinforced and rationalized by culturally derived relativistic definitions of conforming, deviant, and criminal actions, which separate, segregate, and otherwise cause governments at all levels and peoples everywhere to differentially and discriminately enforce laws and punish offenders.
>
> *(Donnermeyer, 2012, p. 289)*

As Friedrichs (2009) reminds us, "The unequal distribution of power and material resources within contemporary societies provides a point of departure for all strains of critical criminology" (p. 210). In other words, critical criminologists, ourselves included, view hierarchical social stratification and inequality along class, racial/ethnic, and gender lines as the major sources of crime and as the key factors that shape societal reactions to violations of legal and social norms (DeKeseredy & Dragiewicz, 2012a; Young, 1988).

What is to be done about crime? Most mainstream criminologists' answers to this question are grounded in the belief that crime is a property of the individual.[3] Thus, they call for responses ranging from coercive counselling therapy to private prisons. Critical criminologists, on the other hand, regard major structural and cultural changes within society as essential to reducing crime and facilitating social justice (DeKeseredy, 2011a). Even so, these progressive scholars are not so naive as to assume that major economic, political, and social transformations will soon occur in patriarchal capitalist societies. After all, even U.S. President Barak Obama, defined as a radical leftist heretic by a sizeable portion of Republican Party members and deemed as a symbol of hope by thousands of liberal U.S. citizens, embraced the highly controversial Patriot Act and has done nothing to try to eliminate the death penalty (Welch, 2012).

It is erroneous to presume that the election of so-called "liberal" politicians like Obama will make much of a difference. In the U.S.A., we are already witnessing the Democratic Party adopting an approach Elliott Currie (1992) defines as "progressive retreatism." This involves embracing parts of conservative policies to win elections. This is, by no means, a new Democratic Party strategy (DeKeseredy, 2009). For example, when Bill Clinton ran for U.S. President in 1992, he declared: "No Republican was going to 'out tough' him on crime" (Chesney-Lind, 2007, p. 212). Recall that he interrupted his New Hampshire primary campaign to preside over the execution of Rickey Ray Rector in his home state of Arkansas (Sherrill, 2001). Thus, for these and other reasons, critical criminologists propose a wide range of progressive initiatives designed to "chip away" at the inequitable status quo (Messerschmidt, 1986).

Provided here is only a brief description of critical criminology and much more is said about this vibrant subfield of criminology in pages to follow. The main objective of this chapter is to introduce four myths about rural crime and challenge long-held assumptions in mainstream criminology about crime in the rural context. First, it is necessary to define the concept "rural."

Definition of rural[4]

Not all rural communities are alike and "Ultimately, the definition of rural communities is arbitrary and open to debate" (Websdale, 1998, p. 40). Even so, following DeKeseredy et al. (2007), rather than overloading a definition of "rural" to reflect social and cultural features that promote idyllic images and suppress the rural realities of crime, we offer a nominal conceptualization of "rural." Here, rural communities are places that have four things in common. First, rural areas have, by definition, smaller population sizes and/or densities. Second, people who live in rural areas are more likely to "know each other's business, come into regular contact with each other, and share a larger core of values than is true of people in urban areas" (Websdale, 1995, p. 102), which variously can be referred to as a higher density of acquaintanceship, collective efficacy, and *Gemeinschaft*, even though each has different but complementary meanings in the sociological and criminological literatures (Donnermeyer, 2012).[5] Collective efficacy is of special concern in a later part of this chapter and it is defined by Sampson, Raudenbush, and Earls (1998) as "mutual trust among neighbors combined with a willingness to act on behalf of the common good, specifically to supervise children and maintain public order" (p. 1). However, we make no claim of a linear relationship between crime and collective efficacy. In fact, in Chapter 3, we reconceptualize collective efficacy as a form of social organization which enables crime. Hence, in this book, we merely recognize that there are levels of mutual trust and that public order exhibits a diversity of expressions among people living at the same place. To do otherwise, we too would backslide into the same fallacies and naïve intellectual concoctions exhibited about the rural and the urban which we seek to crumple up and throw into a trashcan reserved for dichotomies which we hope are never recycled again, either in critical criminology or other subfields of criminology.

Third, in this period of late modernity (Young, 2007), rural communities are much less autonomous than before (Scott, Hogg, Barclay, & Donnermeyer, 2007). For better or worse, the standardization of education, along with other factors, such as new means of electronic communication, have removed some of the unique features of rural culture and narrowed the difference between rural and urban lifestyles (DeKeseredy & Schwartz, 2009; Ritzer, 2013). Although both Tunnell's (2006) reference to Wal-Marting quoted at the beginning of this chapter and Ritzer's (2013) well-known book on McDonaldization refer to globalization's homogenizing influence on how things are made and services are provided, they also refer to something else. It is the growing linkage of rural and urban, and the actualities of and greater potential for a future of growing rural dependency on the urban in forms that truly represent what is meant by "hegemonic." As the reader shall see in Chapter 3, OxyContin comes to the coalfields of Harlan County first as a doctor-administered drug for miners so that coal companies could continue to reap profits and exploit workers, which in turn functions to keep the railroad cars filled for the trains transporting coal to power plants that, in turn, provide cheap power to urban populations, while creating a host of environmental consequences, from acid mine drainage which pollutes local sources of water to carbon emissions which accelerate global warming.

Finally, cultural, social, and economic divides are much more obvious in rural communities than ever before, especially in North America. Transportation systems linking rural and urban areas, the spread of suburbs into formerly rural areas, the presence of industries with absentee ownership, tourism, and the development policies of nation-states – all of these broader structural factors have changed the social and cultural landscape of rural communities (DeKeseredy, Muzzatti, & Donnermeyer, 2013; Donnermeyer et al., 2006).

Myths about rural crime

There are many myths about crime in general, but the bulk of the literature that challenges them is urban based. Consider Bohm and Walker's (2013) *Demystifying Crime and Criminal Justice* and Kappeler and Potter's (2005) *The Mythology of Crime and Criminal Justice*. These are outstanding books, are widely used and read, and should be integral parts of any critical criminologist's library. Nonetheless, conspicuously absent from both of them are chapters on rural issues and the word "rural" is nowhere to be found in the indices. Hopefully, the four myths challenged here will not remain sheltered in a marginalized area of inquiry.

Myth #1: The rural–urban dichotomy[6]

Decades of scholarly work done by criminologists has produced a long list of facile assumptions about the structural and cultural characteristics of urban and rural places and their relationships to crime based on over-generalized interpretations of the writings of sociologists Ferdinand Tönnies (1955) and Lewis Wirth (1938). Tönnies' well-known distinction of *Gemeinschaft–Gesellschaft* is already briefly described in note 5 in this chapter. His arguments were buttressed by the work of Wirth and others associated with the Chicago School of sociology, plus a panoply of scholars in the field of rural sociology who pressed for theoretically sharp and empirically demonstrable differences between the rural and urban populations of the U.S.A. and other Western societies (Brown & Swanson, 2003; Christenson & Garkovich, 1985).

For Wirth, cities were not unique features of modern life because they predate the industrial age. However, he did define the growth of cities and the diffusion of an urban way of life (urbanism) as more distinctively a by-product of the modern era, brought on by technological advances in communication and other technologies, and the inexorable growth in industrialization. In Wirth's (1938) words, "the beginning of what is distinctively modern in our civilization is best signalized by the growth of great cities" (p. 1).

If we fast-forward to this present era, the *Gemeinschaft–Gesellschaft* distinction is still commonly accepted by the general public, many politicians and journalists, and a healthy portion of criminologists, regardless of their political and theoretical orientations. However, we know that not all cities are alike and the same can be said about rural places. Yet, the myth of rural homogeneity is a long-held assumption that continues to hinder the development of rural crime research. It presumed that heterogeneity was a trait intrinsic to the urban milieu, that homogeneity was a trait characteristic of people and groups within specific rural communities, and that all or almost all rural communities were similar.

The reality is far different. Fully 49% of the world's population live in some kind of rural context, from unique rain forest cultures isolated deep in the Amazonia watershed of several South American countries and the Indigenous peoples of the Arctic regions of Scandinavian countries, Russia, Canada, and the U.S. state of Alaska, to the diversity of people and cultures within the millions of villages and small towns scattered throughout Africa, Australia, China, India, and the rest of Asia, Europe, and both North and South America. Within this 49% are economies, cultures, and peoples who create an incredibly diverse array of places and an infinite number of ways in which both conforming and law-abiding behaviors and deviant and criminal behaviors can be expressed. Hence, contrary to popular belief, there are high rates of certain crimes in particular types of rural communities, and these ought to be the focus of criminology as much as diversity among urban places and peoples are already (DeKeseredy et al., 2007).

Myth #2: Collective efficacy = low crime, and social disorganization = high crime

There are scholars, based on a review of the extant literature on informal social control processes in rural communities,[7] who contend that highly injurious crimes (e.g., rape) are atypical in rural areas because they have higher levels of collective efficacy than do metropolitan places. This point is well taken, given that many rural citizens, including agents of social control, share strong ties through kinship systems and friendship networks. As well, residents who live in rural areas are in general less tolerant of many crimes and more likely to strongly support punitive approaches to issues of crime than people from metropolitan areas (DeKeseredy et al., 2007; Donnermeyer et al., 2006; Weisheit, Falcone, & Wells, 2006).

Fairly recent studies (e.g., Barnett & Mencken, 2002; Buffard & Muftić, 2006; Lee, 2008; Osgood & Chambers, 2000, 2003) claim to have found some elements of the antithesis of collective efficacy – social disorganization – in U.S. rural communities, which are associated with arrest rates for youth violence, homicide, fear of crime, and a host of other criminological phenomena.[8] Here, social disorganization is defined as "the inability of a community structure to realize the common values of its residents and maintain effective controls" (Sampson & Groves, 1989, p. 777). However, collective efficacy in rural areas takes different shapes and forms, and is not necessarily restricted to deterring or preventing crimes (Barclay, Donnermeyer, & Jobes, 2004; DeKeseredy & Schwartz, 2009). Moreover, what may appear to outsiders as social disorganization is often "simply a different form of social disorganization if one takes the trouble to look closely" (Wacquant, 1997, p. 346; see also Venkatesh, 2000). For example, 67% of the rural Ohio women interviewed by DeKeseredy, Schwartz, Fagen, and Hall (2006) reported on a variety of ways in which their ex-partners' male peers perpetuated and legitimated separation/divorce assault. Forms of hegemonic patriarchy, like all things studied in criminology, are not sustained in a socio-cultural vacuum of individuals acting mostly on their own, but in networks of similar-minded males. It is not social disorganization that frees up a few so-called deviants to commit crime, but forms of collective efficacy or social organization that allow individuals to learn about and behave in ways that sustain and reinforce their offending.

Similarly, Websdale (1998) uncovered evidence of a powerful "ol' boys" network that serves to dominate and oppress rural Kentucky women. Below a rural Ohio woman describes how such an all-male sexist network and other symptoms of what Websdale refers to as "rural patriarchy" functioned to help stop her from escaping her abusive male partner:

> Another time, after I finally got away from him and I was having these problems. I was, I was on drugs real heavy um, and I was trying to get away from him. He was still calling me. This was just in the last nine months. Um, I called Victim Assistance in my town and um, told them that I had been abused by him. Oh, they kept telling me that they was going to do something about it, and they never did. The one other time I went to Victim Assistance, they told me that um, they were going to question the neighbors and stuff. And the neighbors said that um, you know, they said that the neighbors didn't, didn't see or hear anything. So, they said I didn't have enough, ah, proof. Basically, nothing was ever done. He's a corrections officer in the town that I lived in, and he's friends with the sheriff and whoever else.
>
> *(cited in DeKeseredy & Joseph, 2006, p. 303)*

Biased policing exists everywhere, but a growing body of empirical evidence reveals that it may be more prevalent in rural places (DeKeseredy & Rennison, 2013). Rural police officers tend to be friends with some men who batter their current or former female intimate partners, play sports and drink alcohol with them, and are more likely to refuse to arrest batterers because of what is referred to in Australia as "mateship norms" (Owen, 2012; Scott & Jobes, 2007). For example, Rockell (2013) describes one rural woman, abused by her husband who was a retired member of the state police force and who had convinced her not to file a report because who would his former "troopers" believe, him or her. However, he turned around and filed a complaint and had her arrested when she burned his golf hats and shirts in a trash bin as a way of fighting back. Furthermore, DeKeseredy and Schwartz's (2009) qualitative study of separation/divorce sexual assault in rural Ohio suggests that patriarchal male peer support is more deeply entrenched in rural communities than in urban and suburban ones. This problem is defined as attachments to male peers and the resources they provide that encourage and legitimate woman abuse (DeKeseredy, 1990).[9]

There are other rural studies of crime and social control that call into question the assumptions of social disorganization, including agricultural crime, and two subsets of rural criminology reviewed in Chapter 3 – studies of rural communities and research on substance use among rural populations and drug production and trafficking in rural localities (e.g., Barclay et al., 2004; Edwards & Donnermeyer, 2002; Kaylen & Pridemore, 2013). It can't be emphasized enough that "social organization may facilitate some types of crime even as it constrains others" (Donnermeyer et al., 2006, p. 207).[10] Simply put, disorganization is the wrong word, and, when juxtaposed with organization, presents another false dichotomy that hinders an understanding of rural (and urban) crime. From a critical perspective, and in agreement with Venkatesh (2000) and Wacquant (1997), there is really no such thing as disorganization, only varieties of social structure that facilitate and constrain actions that are defined as either law-abiding or criminal (Donnermeyer, 2012). Collective efficacy, as defined by Sampson (2012), is one-dimensional, focused only on aspects of localized forms of social structure which reduce only certain kinds of crime. In his Presidential address to the American Sociological Association, published in *Criminology*, Sampson (2013) goes so far as to create another false dichotomy by referring to norms that constrain people in neighborhoods from reporting crime (i.e., snitching) as a form of "anti-collective efficacy" rather than simply recognizing that collective efficacy can go both ways when thinking theoretically about crime. Further, regardless of the label, should not this black sheep form of collective efficacy be as much, if not more, the focus of criminology as the other kind?

Myth #3: Rural crime rates were historically low and are only now increasing[11]

Common images in fictional and nonfictional accounts of rural life portray a slower, more peaceful way of life: picturesque farms, Main Street businesses that give personal services to long-standing customers, little school houses with dedicated teachers and studious pupils, and a sheriff that knows everyone by their first name (DeKeseredy & Schwartz, 2009; Hay & Basran, 1992). Further, newspapers and other media often characterize rural people as being nicer to each other than are urban residents (Toughill, 2007). Of course, the media also often depict rural communities as remaining "somewhat behind the times" (Gray, 2007, p. v). There are, indeed, other stereotypes of rural people and life that are addressed in the next section of this chapter. Not surprisingly, the mass media's pictures of the rural–urban divide are frequently inaccurate or gross simplifications. In essence, they are Robinson's (1950) classic expression of the ecological fallacy. For instance, contrary to what many people claim, rural people are not necessarily more likely to help people they know, including relatives, neighbors, or friends (DeKeseredy et al., 2007; Statistics Canada, 2005). There are also North American data that challenge myths about "rural warmth and hospitality" perpetuated by some journalists and others who perceive "small-town folks to be nicer" (Toughill, 2007; Turcotte, 2005). Actually, many rural people are very suspicious of "outsiders" (DeKeseredy, 2007b; Zorza, 2002).

Rural rates of crime in general may be higher than urban rates at particular types of rural places and for specific kinds of crimes (DeKeseredy et al., 2013; Jobes, Barclay, Weinand, & Donnermeyer, 2004). For example, Donnermeyer (2007) found that the official rate of violence for the most rural counties of the United States exceeds those for several dozen metropolitan areas, based on the FBI's *Uniform Crime Report*. In Canada, for the time period 2000 to 2009, the rate of homicide in rural areas (1.92 per 100,000) was higher than the rate for urban areas (1.8) (Hunt, 2012). In Box 1.1, CBC News (2012, p. 2) offers the President of the Canadian Police Association's interpretation of rural homicide and policing in Canada.

Box 1.1 Hidden risks in the country

Rural areas ... have their own perils, says Tom Stamatakis, President of the Canadian Police Association.

"Anecdotally, I would say that on a per capita basis there's a greater likelihood that someone in a rural area is a firearms owner than someone in a city," says Stamatakis.

In most cases, he says, the firearm is registered and has a legitimate use. Many farmers, for example, have rifles to protect themselves and their livestock from predators such as bears and coyotes.

The perils also extend to law enforcement. In the country, lower population density means more wide open spaces. But because there are fewer people, there are also fewer police officers, which means rural officers are often investigating incidents with little or no backup.

"They're dealing with often difficult calls involving intoxicated people and domestic violence situations that that they're having to respond to on their own," says Stamatakis.

Police officers who work in small towns typically form bonds with the local people – often because they also live amongst them. This, too, can have its disadvantages. The lack of anonymity means that a disgruntled resident could easily target an officer.

"There have been many circumstances where police officers are threatened, their property is damaged, their family is threatened because they end up having a negative contact with someone in a small community and that person knows exactly where they live, they know what car they drive, they know where their kids go to school," says Stamatakis.

"Police officers have the tendency to be the kind of people that coach sports teams, that volunteer in the community. They establish some very close ties and relationships in the community," says Stamatakis.

But sometimes when those relationships go sideways, it heightens the risk."

Rural domestic violence is briefly mentioned in Box 1.1, but this social problem is much more serious than the average person can imagine. What's more, there is growing evidence that rural U.S. women are at much greater risk of experiencing intimate violence than are women living in more heavily populated parts of the country. For example, using 1992–2009 National Crime Victimization Survey (NCVS) data, Rennison, DeKeseredy, and Dragiewicz (2012) found that exiting relationships are significantly more dangerous for rural women than for their urban and suburban counterparts. Rural separated women experience intimate rape/sexual assault at rates more than three times higher than their urban counterparts. Rural separated women, too, are raped/sexually assaulted by an intimate partner at rates about 1.6 times higher than similarly situated suburban women. Using the same data set and combining different types of violence together into one dependent variable,[12] Rennison, DeKeseredy, and Dragiewicz (in press) also found that rural divorced and separated females are victimized by intimate partners at rates exceeding separated/divorced urban women. Plus, these researchers uncovered that rural females have a higher rate of all kinds of intimate violence than do urban and suburban females. Exacerbating the plight of rural abused women is that in rural sections of many states, there is widespread acceptance of male-to-female violence and community norms prohibiting victims from publicly talking about their experiences and from seeking social support (DeKeseredy & Schwartz, 2008; Krishnan, Hilbert, & Pace, 2001; Lewis, 2003; Navin, Stockum, & Campbell-Ruggaard, 1993).

Undeniably, for many rural women, the home, a place ostensibly peaceful and violence-free, is a "house of horrors" (Sev'er, 2002). DeKeseredy and Schwartz (2009) speculate that the problem of rural gender violence will only get worse due to threats to the dominant rural hegemonic masculinity, such as the growth of the rural women's movement, tougher drinking and driving laws (Hogg & Carrington, 2006), the crisis in family farming, and the horrification and pornification of rural people in movies, videos, and other media genres. However, this is an empirical issue that can only be effectively addressed empirically, and more in-depth research on rural men is needed to do so (DeKeseredy et al., 2013).

Another fact to keep in mind is that farm operations suffer from higher rates of burglary than do metropolitan businesses (Donnermeyer, Barclay, & Mears, 2011). Rural communities are also not immune from illegal drug use and distribution as documented by recent North American studies (Donnermeyer & Tunnell, 2007; Grant, 2008, 2012; Tunnell, 2004; Weisheit, 2008), and agricultural crimes, such as vandalism and theft, are endemic to the U.S. heartland, as they are in other parts of the world such as Australia (Barclay & Donnermeyer, 2011). Moreover, environmental or "green" crimes, ranging from the illegal trafficking of fauna and flora, to violations of environmental regulations committed by individuals and corporations, and transgressions against hunting laws, frequently occur in rural locations (Clifford, 1998; Donnermeyer, 2012; South & Brisman, 2013; Walters, 2004, 2006; White, 2011, 2013).

As in urban areas, there are "deviant" subcultures in rural communities. Still, like the post-war British youth groups examined by affiliates of the now defunct University of Birmingham Centre for Contemporary Cultural Studies (see Hall & Jefferson, 1977),[13] most of them are resistant and oppositional subcultures, often sown by many decades of poverty and social, cultural, and political marginality (Fisher, 1993; Stough-Hunter, 2010). These oppositional groups express their resistance through music, fashion, language, and behaviors that make them distinctive from the mainstream, an important subject matter for cultural criminologists (e.g., Ferrell, Hayward, & Young, 2008; Muzzatti, 2012). Violations of wildlife and hunting regulations (Forsyth, Gramling, & Wooddell, 1998), varieties of rural-located drug production (Weisheit, 1992, 1993, 2008), and other offenses can be interpreted as forms of behavior based on rural cultural contexts in dependency and resistance.

We could provide an even longer list of crimes that occur in rural communities, including those committed "in the name of hate" (Perry, 2001; see also Chakraborti & Garland, 2004), but it is beyond the scope of this chapter to do so. More comprehensive and in-depth review and assessments of rural crime can be found in a steady stream of books and special issues of journals produced in recent times.[14] Thus, the most important point to consider here is that rural communities are certainly not untouched by serious crimes and that the rates of some types of crime are higher than those for urban and suburban communities.

Myth #4: Which one is it? The Jekyll and Hyde of rural images

There is no more polarized set of images than those associated with rural areas and crime. On the one hand, there is the rural idyll or mystique, a set of images that circumscribe rural areas as free of crime and safe for "all creatures, great and small" (the title of the fictional stories about a veterinarian and quaint rustic village and farm life in rural North York-shire). On the other hand, there is the image of rural as a dangerous place, where demented, toothless sociopaths lie in wait with chainsaws for unsuspecting victims, who more often than not are hapless sojourn-ers from cities and suburbs.

The rural idyll or rural mystique is a series of idealized stereotypes about rural communities (Bell, 2006; Cloke & Little, 1997; Danbon, 1991; Logan, 1996; Philo, 1997; Short, 2006). In an earlier work, Rohrer and Douglas (1969), based on Mannheim's (1954) definition of ideology as a "conscious disguise" of reality, described the agrarian ideo-logy in the U.S.A. as a set of three beliefs shared by many and derived from the articulate writings of the country's third President, Thomas Jefferson. The first is that farmers, and by extension, rural people in general, are more independent and self-sufficient. Today, this myth finds its expression frequently in Country and Western music, such as the mythology embedded in the popular Hank Williams Jr. song from the early 1980s titled "A Country Boy Can Survive."

The next linchpin of the agrarian ideology states that all nonfarm occupations are reliant on agriculture for their existence because, without food, there could not be any other kind of economic activity, much less music, the arts, education and all of the other features we associate with civilization (Rohrer & Douglas, 1969). Hence, it is a form of agricultural determinism. Even though this belief fails to recog-nize that its takes a village of engineers to design and build expensive tractors and combines for farmers, the belief in the fundamental nature of agriculture on which all else in a society is based is a one-way belief that persists.

The third belief stems from the first two and is the most directly rel-evant of the three for images of rural and urban crime. It is the idea that agricultural life is natural and good, and hence, by extension, rural places are inhabited by people who are more law-abiding, ethical, and moral than the urban populace. This part of the ideology is not only commonly accepted in countries like the United States and Great Britain, but seeps into the mindset of the criminology community through flippant acceptance (hence, misinterpretation – Donnermeyer, 2007b, 2012) of Tönnies' *Gemeinschaft–Gesellschaft*, Wirth's (1938) classic statement of urbanism, and the concepts of social disorganization and collective efficacy, and the newest label of all, anti-collective efficacy.

Frank's (2003) analysis of newspaper coverage of violence in small towns of the U.S.A. demonstrates the sustainability of the rural idyll, even in the face of incidents that clearly belie its truthfulness. He identified four themes, namely, that rural residents know each other, that rural towns have a slower pace (i.e., are "sleepy"), that rural people feel safe and do not see a need to lock their doors, and that "terrible" events do not happen in rural settings. Hence, when murder, school shootings and other forms of violence take place in a rural community, the headlines proclaim the incident as of an exceptional nature. Crime, when it occurs in rural communities and to rural people, is an aberration, maybe even an "urban invasion," ignoring the reality that it is the place-based expression of an established social organization and an enduring structural inequality, reinforced by localized cultural context or norms, values, and beliefs (Liepins, 2000).

Mass media in the U.S.A. and many other countries frequently emphasize tight-knit communities, strong family ties, and rugged individualism as hallmarks of rural areas. As Lichter, Amundson, and Lichter (2003) put it:

> There can be little doubt that American mass media have played a significant role in building and decorating these frames. From the late 19th-century dime novels that depicted winning the Wild West, to the "horse operas" that dominated the early days of television entertainment, to the big screen epics of John Wayne and John Huston, entertainment has idolized the rugged individual battling nature and human venality in the untamed west. More recent pop culture products like the television series *The Waltons* and *Little House on the Prairie*, along with cinematic hits like *Places in the Heart* and *The River* have presented warmer, more personal tales of

rural Americans overcoming adversity and upholding traditional values. Even fluff like *Petticoat Junction*, *Green Acres*, and the *Dukes of Hazzard* have played a role in our collective associations with rural America.

(p. 1)

Many people assume that little crime occurs in rural U.S. communities, an assumption heavily fueled by the media, lay conversations, and even criminological research which, as stated earlier, is urban-centric. Similarly, most people and the media view rural communities as safer than urban localities (Carrington, 2007; Donnermeyer, DeKeseredy, & Dragiewicz, 2011). According to Canadian newspaper reporter Theresa Boyle (2007), "After all, conventional wisdom holds that the big, bad city is the root of all evil.... Small towns are supposed to be peaceful and serene" (p. A3). True, many small towns fit this description, but the reality is that rural communities are not less criminogenic than urban places.

Images of the rural as bucolic places free of crime, and of rural people as more honest and more law-abiding, while urban places and people are the opposite, can be found frequently in the popular imagination, the media, and literary works of many societies (Cloke, Hogg, & Carrington, 2003; Lichter et al., 2003; Short, 2006; Willits, Bealer, & Timbers, 1990). Yet, there is the "other" side as well – the Jekyll to the Hyde – of rural localities sensationalized as places where senseless acts of violence occur because it seems to be woven into the very fabric of the culture. Bell (1997) refers to it as the anti-idyll, and it too finds its way into the criminology literature, albeit in a softer form, such as the "subculture of violence" thesis (Nelsen, Corzine, & Huff-Corzine, 1994; Nisbett, 1993).

Often lost in scholarly, media, and other types of discussion of racism, sexism, and segregation is the plight of rural people, especially those who live in Southern Appalachia.[15] As Foster and Hummel (1997) correctly point out, "region, unlike gender and race, lacks sufficient political and economic salience to be cast as a national issue" (p. 157). Furthermore, what these two sociologists argued over 15 years ago still holds true today: Southern Appalachian mountain residents and many other rural people are commonly and negatively stereotyped as "hillbillies."[16]

Certainly, the media plays a key role in this stereotyping. Television shows such as *The Beverly Hillbillies*, some comic strips (e.g., *Li'l Abner*), and myriad joke books depict typical rural men as "wearing the obligatory floppy hat, ragged shirts, and tattered baggy overalls" (Foster & Hummel, 1997, p. 160). They are also frequently portrayed as carrying muzzle-load rifles, sucking on corncob pipes, and drinking moonshine (DeKeseredy & Schwartz, 2009; Williamson, 1995). Sadly, hillbilly caricatures encourage people to consider "southern mountaineers as backward, lazy, dumb, and unable to cope with the modern world" (Inge, 1989, p. 915), images as grossly stereotypical as their Hyde-like opposites perpetuated by Hank Williams Jr. and in other Country and Western songs.

To make matters worse, most media stories about rural life prioritize men's experiences over those of women and rarely feature women as community leaders or family breadwinners. Rather, such stories usually characterize rural women, especially those who live in Appalachia as either hardened, asexual grandmothers or sexual objects with large breasts, curvaceous hips, halter tops, and skimpy, frayed denim short-shorts (DeKeseredy & Schwartz, 2009; Foster & Hummel, 1997).

There are yet two other sets of negative stereotypes about rural people. One is the "rural slasher," such as the killers featured in the popular films *Texas Chainsaw Massacre*, *Friday the 13th* and its sequels, and *The Hills Have Eyes*. Such "hillbilly horror" films generate much profit and are deeply embedded in popular youth discourse. The second set of stereotypes features the pornification of rural people, especially women, on the Internet and in other media. Horrification is the persistent depiction of any group of people within a particular society as the perpetrators and/or victims of extreme forms of violence, in various visual, print, and other mass media genres, and its distribution. Similarly, pornification is the persistent depiction of any group of people within a particular society as the perpetrators and/or victims of extreme forms of sexual behavior and exploitation, including violent and racist portrayals of heterosexual sex, in various media, and its distribution and use within society (DeKeseredy et al., 2013).

Media that horrify and pornify rural culture are intimately linked for two reasons. First, the horrification and pornification of rural culture is normalized and mainstreamed. Second, they contribute equally to the masking or "conscious disguise" of real issues about crime, violence, and gender relations in rural contexts that were described in the previous section of this chapter.

First, let's consider in detail what horror movies say about the rural. What all hillbilly horror and rural slasher films have in common is that, in Bell's (1997) words, they trade on "assorted cultural myths ... of inbreeding, insularity, backwardness, and sexual perversion (especially incest and bestiality)" (p. 96). Another common theme is innocent city folk, especially youth, meeting "an alien culture where the norms of their own society count for nothing. Their innocent picture of the countryside – as a place passed through or to holiday in – is forever bloodied" (p. 99).

Bell notes that rural slasher films such as *Friday the 13th* are deemed by some scholars to be important commentaries on U.S. culture and to represent a "progressive, transgressive, and radical critique" (p. 97).[17] In sharp contrast, Stephen King (1981), the best-selling horror author, argues that the rural slasher film (and other horror movies):

> is really as conservative as an Illinois Republican in a three-piece suit; that its main purpose is to reaffirm the virtues of the norm by showing us what awful things happen to people who venture into taboo lands. Within this framework of most horror tales we find a moral code so strong it would make a Puritan smile.
>
> *(p. 395)*

From a feminist standpoint, we agree with King even though his inter-pretation is not informed by gender studies. For example, Welsh's (2010) study of 50 English-language slasher films released between 1960 and 2009, such as the remake of *Friday the 13th* and the original version of *Texas Chainsaw Massacre*, shows that female victims were much more likely to have sexual relations than female survivors who abstained from sex. In an earlier study, Welsh (2009) found that female characters were significantly more likely than males to be hurt by a broad range of violent behaviors, including various types of psycho-logical terror and confinement. Definitely, brutal violence as a punish-ment of "immoral" females who violate patriarchal gender norms is a major theme in rural slasher films (Clover, 1992; Cowan & O'Brien,

1990; Linz, Donnerstein, & Penrod, 1984; Welsh, 2010). We and Stephen Muzzatti (see DeKeseredy et al., 2013) contend that *Friday the 13th* and similar films contribute to keeping a woman "in her place." As well, stigmatizing women who violate gender norms helps groups of men rationalize their own deviant or criminal behaviors (DeKeseredy & Schwartz, 2013; Schur, 1984).

More recently, we see a new type of female victim in some rural horror movies. While violence against her is also a punishment for violating patriarchal gender norms, she is not killed, beaten, psychologically terrorized, confined, or tortured strictly because of her sexuality or sexual behavior. Instead, she is harmed because she is upwardly mobile and has exited an intimate relationship with a patriarchal, working-class, rural man. Note that in "real life," many women who exit or who try to leave intimate, heterosexual relationships are at high risk of being murdered or of suffering non-lethal violence (DeKeseredy, 2011b). As Polk (2003) reminds us, "Time and time again the phrase 'if I can't have you, no one will' echoes through the data on homicide in the context of sexual intimacy" (p. 134). In actual fact, in the U.S.A., close to 50% of men on death row for domestic murder killed their wives or lovers in retaliation for leaving (Rapaport, 1994; Stark, 2007).[18]

The above female character is prominently featured in the 2011 film *Shark Night 3D*. Sara is one of seven Tulane University undergraduates who take a vacation at her family's home on a private lake in the Louisiana Gulf. To make a long story short, Dennis, Sara's old boyfriend, his friend Red, and the local sheriff put sharks in the lake. Dennis is angry that Sara has left him and uses the sharks to seek revenge, but this is not the sole motive for using them.[19] Of course, scattered throughout the film are brutal scenes of violence too graphic to be described here.

This film, like rural slashers, "amplifies the urban–rural divide" and as is the case in *Friday the 13th*, the deaths of innocent young city people are calculated acts of revenge. Nonetheless, what makes Sara distinct from the female victims of violence in other rural horror movies is that she was raised in the community where the horror takes place and, again, she distanced herself from her working-class boyfriend (and her town). She was punished for resisting patriarchal dominance and control, as well as for seeking a higher socio-economic status than that of Dennis. Sara, though, survives at the end of the movie, but there is a major difference between her and female survivors in rural slasher films. As Cowan and O'Brien (1990) discovered in their study, "The female survivors were not only the 'good girls,' but also more androgynous, less inane, and less physically attractive than the nonsurviving females" (p. 195). Sara, on the other hand, is conveniently attractive and is sometimes featured in a bikini.

Shark Night 3D constitutes a somewhat radical departure from its rural horror predecessors. Nevertheless, many of the new horror movies released over the past few years are simply remakes of older ones (e.g., *The Hills Have Eyes*), which continue to reinforce images of rural people as inbred or psychotic men in bib overalls. Additional damage is done by films that feature these "psychotic hayseeds" (Sconce, 1995). For example, after watching slasher films, college men have less sympathy for rape victims, see them as less injured, and are more likely to endure the resilient myth that women enjoy rape (Cowan & O'Brien, 1990; DeKeseredy et al., in press; Malamuth & Check, 1981). Internet pornography, too, perpetuates and legitimates negative stereotypes of rural people, especially women, and it buttresses rape myths.

Although a very different form of media, pornographic depictions using rural settings and rural characters have, in general, the same consequences as rural horror movies. They perpetuate stereotypes, that is, they are constructed disguises which mask other rural realities (Mannheim, 1954). Today, pornography is mainly "gonzo – that genre which is all over the Internet and is today one of the biggest moneymakers for the industry – which depicts hard-core, body-punishing sex in which women are demeaned and debased" (Dines, 2010, p. xi). Millions of people around the world routinely consume gonzo and other forms of pornography (DeKeseredy, 2013). In fact, there is ample evidence that men who do not view or read it are atypical (DeKeseredy & Schwartz, 2013). Keep in mind that every second, over 28,258 Internet users view pornography (DeKeseredy & Olsson, 2011; Zerbisias, 2008), and the vast majority of them are men and boys (Bridges & Jensen, 2011).

There are over four million pornography sites on the Internet (Dines, 2010), with as many as 10,000 added every week (DeKeseredy & Olsson, 2011). Additionally, worldwide pornography revenues from a variety of sources (e.g., Internet, sex shops, hotel rooms, etc.) recently topped $97 billion. This is more than the combined revenues of Microsoft, Google, Amazon, eBay, Yahoo!, Apple, Netflix, and Earthlink (DeKeseredy, 2013; Zerbisias, 2008). More recent evidence of the growth of pornography is the emergence of "tubes," such as YouPorn, XTube, and PornoTube, all based on the widely used and popular YouTube. YouPorn had 15 million users after launching in 2006 and was growing at a monthly rate of 37.5% (Mowlabocus, 2010). Undoubtedly, cyberporn is "the quietest big business in the world" (Slayden, 2010, p. 57).

Closely associated with the increasingly profitable and accessible nature of pornography is an enormous increase in violent and racist materials (Barron & Kimmel, 2000; Jensen, 2007), which have become mainstreamed in the industry (Bridges & Anton, in press). The study by Bridges, Wosnitzer, Scharrer, Sun and Liberman (2010) of 304 scenes in 50 of the most popular pornographic DVDs confirms this point. Nearly 90% contained physical aggression (mainly spanking, gagging, and slapping) and roughly 50% included verbal aggression, primarily name-calling. Not surprisingly, males constituted most of the perpetrators and the targets of their physical and verbal aggression were "overwhelmingly female." Furthermore, the female targets often showed pleasure or responded neutrally to male aggression. Making the data uncovered by Bridges et al. (2010) more troubling is the observation by Brosi, Foubert, Bannon and Yandell (2010):

> [A]s the pornography industry grows and seeks to satisfy its increasingly large customer base, it has continuously innovated its products and materials in a direction of more extreme, violent, "edgy," material, often featuring underage actors and scenes depicting a wide variety of dehumanizing behaviors not heretofore seen.
>
> *(p. 27)*

Despite, in general, being more politically conservative than metropolitan and suburban areas (Kay, 2011), rural communities, too, have become "pornified" (Paul, 2005). Scott Bergthold, a U.S. lawyer who helps small towns fight "adult business," told *Los Angeles Times* reporter Stephanie Simon (2004, p. 2), "Rural communities never thought they'd have to deal with what they perceived to be a big-city problem."

Obviously, things have changed, as hard-core porn has now "hit the heartland." For example, the Lion's Den chain now has an "adult super-store" in Quaker City, Ohio, population 563, because of its proximity to an interstate highway (DeKeseredy & Schwartz, 2009). At least a third of their stores are located off a U.S. interstate highway and in or near towns of 16,000 or fewer residents (Howlett, 2012). Kat Sunlove, an adult movie actress turned lobbyist working for the Free Speech Center, views these stores (sometimes referred to as "freeway porn stores") and the pornification of rural highways as "capitalism at its best.... This is a transformed industry, and businesses are just following the market" (cited in Howlett, 2012, p. 1).

Not only are businesses following the market, but also rural consumers. For instance, there is evidence that rural boys consume pornography more than do their urban counterparts (Betowski, 2007; DeKeseredy & Olsson, 2011). Further, the states with the most pornography subscription rates in the U.S.A. (e.g., Mississippi) have large rural populations (Edleman, 2009). As DeKeseredy and Schwartz (2009) found, many female victims of separation/divorce sexual assault indicate their partners were frequent consumers of pornography.[20]

Thousands of what DeKeseredy and Schwartz (2009, p. 6) refer to as "the false images of rural life" are found on countless cyberporn sites. All one has to do is simply conduct a Google search using the words "rural gonzo porn." A search using the phrase "farm girl porn" on Google reported 16,000,000 results on September 11, 2012 and major examples of film titles listed are *Two Outdoor Sluts* and *Anal in the Farm* (DeKeseredy et al., 2013). Big breasts, halter tops, and frayed denim short-shorts are worn by most of the younger women in these movies and many of them are portrayed as farmers' daughters. Moreover, almost all of the sex acts take place outside or in barns. Similar images of women appear in thousands of Internet farm girl porn "comics" or "cartoons."

Similar to characters in scores of rural horror movies, many of the rural people featured in the cyberporn comics are characterized as inbreds or "hicks." Actually, incest is a common theme that runs throughout many rural farm girl porn cartoon sites. One prime example is Jab Comix's cartoon *Real Hicks Get Naughty*, which depicts a nephew having sexual intercourse with his aunt and then having anal sex with his sister.

Like pornographic videos filmed in urban and suburban areas and pornographic comics and cartoons that use these areas as backdrops, another thing all forms of rural pornography have in common is that the women featured in these media are

> represented as passive and as slavishly dependent upon men. The role of female characters is limited to the provision of sexual services to men. To the extent that women's sexual pleasure is represented at all, it is subordinated to that of men and is never an end itself as is the sexual pleasure of men. What pleases men is the use of their bodies to satisfy male desires. While the sexual objectification of women is common to all pornography, in which women characters are killed, tortured, gang-raped, mutilated, bound, and otherwise abused, as a means of providing sexual stimulation or pleasure to the male characters.
>
> *(Longino, 1980, p. 42)*

Women are not the only ones harmed by rural pornography and horror. These media, combined with hillbilly stereotypes and caricatures in other elements of popular culture (e.g., television shows and mainstream movies), lower many rural people's status, regardless of their sex and age, and they pathologize their culture. Unfortunately, despite the proliferation of university-based rural and Appalachian studies programs, a sizeable portion of the U.S. population continues to hold rural people in low regard and much profit is to be gained by doing so (Chapman, 2009; Eller, 2008; Foster & Hummel, 1997).

The media is an integral part of the "criminology of the other," one that depicts criminals as "threatening, excluded outcasts" (Drake, 2011; Garland, 1996). In other words, criminals are portrayed as "bogeymen" (Irwin, 1985), "demons," or very distinct from those whom Hirschi (1969) refers to as having a strong social bond to conventional society (DeKeseredy, 2013). This myth that "criminals" are fundamentally different from "noncriminals" has a long history. Prior to the late 1700s, most European legal authorities thought that supernatural forces caused crime and people to act like the cannibals in *Texas Chainsaw Massacre*. People officially designated as deviant were seen as sinners who either fell from grace with God (for example, moral failure) or were possessed by the devil or other evil spirits (DeKeseredy & Schwartz, 1996). Even in this current era, some religious people and groups claim the devil influences crime (Vold, Bernard, Snipes, & Gerould, 2009). Nevertheless, we now have a more sophisticated understanding of crime, but many people continue to view the causes of crime within the individual.[21] Moreover, for more than two centuries, scholars who adhered to this notion have attempted to identify the "criminal man" based on genetics, personalities, or group membership. Despite failing to scientifically achieve this goal (Felson, 2006), the strongly held belief that those who break the law are innately "bad" still persists (Young, 2011).

There is ample evidence refuting the myths that the major threats to urban people visiting rural areas are psychotic, inbred serial killers and that rural farm women are dumb nymphomaniacs. Yet, these myths carry on. There are several reasons for this. One, of course, is that the media buttresses these myths in a variety of ways in order to make a profit. One method is the creation and distribution of hillbilly horror films. In films of these types:

> Psychotic super-male criminals generally possess an evil, cunning intelligence and superior strength, endurance, and stealth. Crime is an act of twisted, lustful revenge or a random act of irrational violence. A historical trend has been to present psychotic criminals as more violent and bloodthirsty and to show their crimes more graphically. As the most popular construction of criminality, the psychopathic criminal clearly supports the individually focused biological and psychological theories to the exclusion of other criminological perspectives. Crime is innate, an act of nature gone bad and not society's fault.
>
> *(Surette, 2011, p. 64)*

Why does the media's horrification/pornification of rural culture continue to flourish? DeKeseredy (2013) offers a feminist answer to this question. For him, highly degrading and grossly distorted media representations of male-to-female violence serve the interests of men who abuse female intimates. Such images support the myths that sexual assaults, femicides, and beatings are committed only by pathological "sex fiends" and that women enjoy "rough sex" depicted in cyber porn (Beckett & Sasson, 2000). Many scholars would disagree with this radical feminist interpretation and assert that what DeKeseredy is actually describing is the consequence of viewing hillbilly horror and rural porn.[22] Certainly, the interests of abusive and patriarchal men are served, but the media critiqued here are highly profitable and therefore many would argue that this is the key determinant. Again, porn generates huge profits and so do rural slasher films.

Summary

Despite the plethora of criminological research readily available, it is truly amazing how little is known about rural crimes and societal reactions to them within the broader academic criminological community. Such selective inattention definitely contributes to the resilience of the myths about rural crime and rural culture examined in this chapter. As well, it seems that degrading stereotypes about rural people continue to be widely accepted. Some rural criminologists even contend that "hillbillies" or people commonly referred to as "white trash" are more detested than other minorities in the U.S.A. As Weisheit et al. (2006, pp. 38–39) correctly point out:

> It is hard to imagine many jokes about rednecks or white trash being tolerated if some other groups were substituted in the joke. When Paula Jones accused President Clinton of sexual harassment, comments about white trash were freely dispensed. James Carville, former adviser to the president, was quoted as saying, "Drag a hundred dollar bill through the trailer court and there's no telling what you will find"; a reporter for *Newsweek* said on television that Jones had a reputation for being "just some sleazy woman with big hair coming out of the trailer parks"; and *U.S. News and World Report* described Paula Jones' home town as a "land of big hair and tight jeans and girls whose dreams soar no further than a stint at a hairdressers' school" [Lee, 1997, p. 11; Thurman, 1997, p. 3].

Critical criminology, though, is playing a strong role in challenging myths and stereotypes about rural people and communities. This progressive school of thought's emphasis on various forms of inequality, plus a sharp focus on the specific contexts of crime, overturn overly broad generalities about rural places and lower crime (and urban places and higher crime), cleansing scholars' minds of decades of stereotypes about both the countryside and the city, and allowing one to focus more on the relationship of forms of social organization and context to criminal behaviors (Donnermeyer, 2012; Young, 1992). By linking macro- and micro-level analyses, the essence of any sound critical criminological approach, the old dichotomies that have so long hampered the development of rural criminology and limited the breadth of mainstream criminology will end.

We are reminded of Liepins (2000) attempt to redefine the concept of the rural community by recognizing that all communities, both large and small, are the product of the interplay between spaces/structures, practices and behavior of the people who live contiguously, and the meanings they assign to these spaces and structures. By linking the macro and micro, and by considering the localized expressions of structural inequalities and segmentation, along with networks in which people live, work, and play (including how they engage in criminal activities), we can achieve a deeper understanding of rural crime, add breadth to critical criminology, and challenge fundamental notions about crime and place which for too long have been less than accurate staples within mainstream criminology. We hope to achieve one more thing – a perspective about crime at rural places that looks well beyond the four mythologies.

2

THINKING CRITICALLY ABOUT RURAL CRIME

> Theories are always based on the assumption that crime follows patterns and that uncovering those patterns is an important step in eventually understanding crime. Many of our basic models of crime don't seem to fit rural areas, suggesting critical flaws in the models.
>
> *(Weisheit et al., 2006, p. 11)*

Criminology was not always urban-centric, even though it did first develop in countries of Europe and North America, which were among the first to industrialize and whose urban populations became the majority soon after the 20th century began. In fact, as Weisheit et al. (2006) note:

> The earliest theories in American criminology were characterized by a distinctly nonurban perspective, reflecting the predominantly rural, small-town backgrounds of most of the pioneering theorists in sociology and criminology (Laub, 1983; Mills, 1943). In 1900, over 70% of Americans lived in rural areas and what we now call suburbs hardly existed (Hobbs & Stoops, 2002). Rural communities and towns were implicitly taken as the natural social form, providing the stable reference point from which urban life could be analyzed as an interesting deviation.
>
> *(p. 10)*

What accounted for the dramatic shift in criminological focus? The world is multivariate, and single-factor explanations cannot adequately account for the current state of criminological theorizing. Nevertheless, it is safe to say that as contemporary society became more urbanized, so did academic criminology, which is one of the key determinants of what Hogg and Carrington (2006) refer to as "sociological and criminological urbanism" (p. 1). Arguably, the trend toward crafting and testing theories of crime in metropolitan areas took flight after the 1950s (Weisheit et al., 2006), but from a well-built intellectual runway constructed in the first half of the 20th century and even extending back into the previous century.

Concurrently, "abstracted empiricism has expanded on a level which would have surely astonished Mills himself" (Young, 2011, p. viii).[1] Further, the variety of data available to criminologists through official government agencies, from a census or population bureau to the police and criminal justice agencies, is astounding. Although in many countries, such as the U.S.A., a similar entourage of statistical information is also available for rural areas (as we shall see in the two topics of focus in Chapter 3), we cannot help but link the rise of abstracted empiricism with the growth of an urban-centric criminology.

Sadly, much of what characterizes criminology in the U.S.A. and many other countries is "voodoo" or "so-what? criminology" (Currie, 2007; Young, 2004). Such criminology involves doing a-theoretical, quantitative research on relatively minor issues and presenting the findings in a fashion unintelligible to all who have not passed advanced statistics courses. It is not, however, statistics *sui generis* that are the issue, it is the application of statistics and theoretical concepts, the balance between them, and how findings or results are interpreted. What such narrowness of focus does is fail to consider larger, conceptual issues.

Although, much less positivistic than mainstream U.S. criminology, rural criminology is, for the most part, stuck in a theoretical rut. For example, no other theory has been adopted more by rural criminologists than social disorganization theory. Consider, too, that nowhere to be found in Donnermeyer's (2007) comprehensive review of theories applied to rural crime or offerings that have the potential to help explain this social problem are critical criminological perspectives. This is not to say, however, that rural criminology is entirely mainstream. If it was, then we would not have written this book! The good news is that a spate of critical criminological books, journal articles, and book chapters have been published since the early part of this decade and more such contributions are destined to emerge soon.

The main objective of this chapter is to offer a brief history of rural critical criminology and to review new progressive ways of thinking critically about crime and social control. We focus on intimate partner violence and agricultural crime to show how critical perspectives advance our understanding of crime in the rural context and go further by posing challenges that we hope will revise mainstream criminology. In the next chapter, we continue our use of a critical interpretation by reinterpreting community-focused rural crime research, studies of substance use, drug manufacturing and trafficking in the rural context, and agricultural crime.

The roots of critical rural criminology

As rural critical criminology matures, hopefully, this won't be the last telling of its history. Regardless, an unknown number of readers may disagree with our account. This is not a problem for reasons offered in Raymond Michalowski's (1996) story of critical criminology: "This is all to the good. I increasingly suspect that we can best arrive at useful truth by telling and hearing multiple versions of the same story" (p. 9). Our version begins with William Chambliss' (1964, 1973) seminal study of the original vagrancy laws, which is also considered by other progressive scholars as marking the birth of rural critical criminology (Coventry & Palmer, 2008).

The original vagrancy laws

In North America, Europe, and other parts of the world, large corporations, with the assistance of governments, are staging massive assaults on working- and middle-class people who are struggling to maintain their wages and to keep their jobs. As critical criminologist Richard Quinney (1977) pointed out when he identified himself as a structural Marxist:[2]

> The capitalist system must be continuously reproduced. This is accomplished in a variety of ways, ranging from the establishment of ideological hegemony to the further exploitation of labor, from

the creation of public policy to the coercive repression of the population. Most explicitly, the *state* secures the capitalist order. Through various schemes and mechanisms, then, the capitalist state is able to dominate.

(pp. 43–44, emphasis in original)

Business or economic elites have not only played a major role in the creation of labor laws, but they also helped create a healthy portion of criminal laws, such as the original vagrancy laws in England. One of the key reasons for designing these statutes was the Black Death that occurred during the middle of the 14th century. This was a cholera plague that reduced Europe's population by as much as 50% (Chambliss, 1993). Consequently, England experienced a major shortage of cheap labor. Additionally, to increase their standard of living, laborers left land estates to seek higher wages in new industrial towns and the chances of getting caught were minimal at best. This created major problems for landowners because they could not offer competitive salaries. Hence, the Crown sided with the landowners and created vagrancy laws that made it a criminal offense to refuse work or to leave a job without permission:

> Every man and woman, of what condition he be, free or bond, able in body, and within the age of three-score years, not living in merchandise nor exercising any craft, nor having of his own whereon to live, nor proper land whereon to occupy himself, and not serving any other, if he in convenient service (his estate considered) be required to serve, shall be bounded to serve him which shall him require.... And if any refuse, he shall on conviction by two true men ... be committed to gaol till he find surety to serve. And if any workman or servant, of what estate or condition he be, retained in any man's service, do depart from the said service without reasonable cause or license, before the term agreed on, he shall have pain of imprisonment.

(cited in Chambliss, 1993, p. 47)

Echoing similar sentiments to today's "right-to-work" laws, which reduce the power of workers to organize for better wages and benefits and endow economic elites and corporations greater power to exploit labor and increase corporate profits, the vagrancy statutes of older times were, as Chambliss (1973) puts it, "designed for one express purpose: to force laborers to accept employment at a low wage in order to insure the landowner an adequate supply of labor at a price he could afford to pay" (p. 435). These laws, though, became useless after the breakup of feudalism and the new economic dependence on commerce and trade (Chambliss, 1993). So, after the turn of the 16th century, the vagrancy laws shifted their focus to "rogues," "vagabonds," and to any person who "can give no reckoning of how he lawfully gets his living" (Chambliss, 1973, p. 436).

In the U.S.A. during the late nineteenth and early twentieth centuries, vagrancy laws were used by the police as a "catch-all to permit the police to deal with the poor at their discretion" (Chambliss, 1993, p. 49). Still, the main targets of these laws were, not surprisingly, African Americans (Kennedy, 1997; Mills, 2012). In the days after the U.S. Civil War, rural blacks were controlled through a combination of "Jim Crow" laws of state-sponsored segregation and an agricultural system known as sharecropping. Sharecropping was highly exploitative because black agriculturalists did not own the land they farmed, and were charged a rent for the price of the supplies (seeds, etc.) provided by the landowner once the crops were sold at market. Landowners could set whatever price they wanted, reaping profits for themselves and keeping blacks at the lowest end of an exploitative system of social class (Pfeffer, 1984). Because slavery was abolished, however, even these exploited blacks could migrate to northern states, where factory work and better living conditions existed, even though there was much segregation by neighborhood, and discrimination against blacks in schools and other institutions as well. Known as the "Great Migration," they did so in the millions (Lemann, 1991: Zeiderman, 2006). Today, U.S. vagrancy laws are much narrower and more clearly defined, but they remain a response to rural-to-urban migration of blacks and other minorities to U.S. cities as their populations and economies grew through decades of industrialization, and they are still frequently employed to target and warehouse what Marxist scholar Stephen Spitzer (2008) identifies as "social junk" or people who fail to, are unable to, or who refuse to "participate in the roles supportive of capitalist society" (p. 72).

Chambliss' study is trail-blazing on many levels. He did not continue down the rural critical criminological path, but he advanced critical criminology in general and did much for young progressive scholars seeking to develop radical alternatives to mainstream perspectives on the state and law. He is especially well known for creating structural contradictions theory[3] and for being the first critical criminologist to become the President of the American Society of Criminology. Structural contradictions theory is a variant of Marxist legal theory. It "sees law creation as a process aimed at the resolution of contradictions, conflicts and dilemmas which are inherent in the structural of a historical period" (Chambliss, 1986, p. 30).

The contemporary roots of rural criminology

Many critical criminologists who followed in Chambliss' footsteps, especially those who produced theories of crime and its control in the 1970s and early 1980s, relied on Marxist analyses of capitalist society (Matthews, 2012). Perhaps because they were so concerned with economic structures, these scholars took a "gender-blind" or "male-centered" approach to criminological studies (Gelsthorpe & Morris, 1988; Mooney, 2012). Some of the most widely cited of these radical works ignored gender, sexuality, and women.[4] As repeatedly stated, this criticism can also be easily directed at the overwhelming majority of orthodox or mainstream criminologists (DeKeseredy, 2011a).

As well, critical criminologists mostly committed the same mistake as mainstream criminology, by focusing largely on the urban to the exclusion of the rural when place-based theories and research was conducted. Even the early work by Tönnies, who is automatically considered an early theorist of place and crime, was not focused on place per se, but rather the place from which criminals came, and how their "wills" or motivation for committing different sorts of offenses varied by place (Deflem, 1999). He claimed that essential will, associated with a *Gemeinschaft*-like form of social organization, was related to murder and other forms of violent behavior (as well as perjury and arson); while arbitrary will, which is connected with a *Gesellschaft* form of social organization, explains more rationally planned types of crime, such as theft, con and fraud, and robbery (Deflem, 1999). From Tönnies' point of view, the dichotomy is trans-historical, that is, communities were made up of a mix of both types of will as exhibited by its citizens.

Unfortunately, Tönnies' dichotomy was misinterpreted to a considerable extent, so that by the time the Chicago School of sociology was beginning its empirical studies of crime in the first half of the 20th century, the focus was squarely on the heterogeneity and other so-called *Gesellschaft* features of urban neighborhoods (Deflem, 1999). Even though the Chicago School developed at a time that was not too far from the frontier days of violence and lawlessness in the U.S.A., the myths about rurality and lack of crime had formed. Studies of crime within the urban milieu already had cornered the intellectual market in criminology.

Adding to the neglect of the rural was the influence of a comprehensive review of scholarship about rural society, including rural–urban comparisons of official crime rates from the U.S.A. and several other European countries by Sorokin, Zimmerman, and Galpin (1931). They concluded that "the number of crimes or offences is greater in the cities than in the country," that "cities produce a proportionately greater number of offenders than does the country," and "in general the agricultural population is one of the least criminal of all occupational classes" (pp. 266–267). Hence, most rural sociologists turned away from inquiries about crime to other issues, including rural and community development, agriculture and food, and the demography of places. It is still ignored today. For instance, a recent anthology of contemporary rural studies, edited by two prominent rural sociologists, David L. Brown and Louis E. Swanson (2003), not only includes nothing related to crime and deviance, but largely ignores issues related to gender, racism, and human rights.

Throughout the first 80 years of the 20th century, rural crime research was infrequent and scattered. Rural, when mentioned, was mostly the "straight man" to be juxtaposed to the conditions that cause crime and that were falsely assumed to exist only or mostly within urban places. Some exceptions did exist, but did not help much. Smith (1933) wrote a comprehensive account of rural crime in the U.S.A., but apparently it did little to change the headstrong urban bias of criminology, in part because his emphasis was on the movement of gangsters to rural hideouts, and the impact of the automobile on the urban-to-rural diffusion of crime. Vold (1941) was careful to point out that homicide rates in the rural portions of some states exceeded those in the major cities of other states. Clinard's (1942, 1944) work on rural criminal offenders highlighted both similarities between and differences from urban offenders, as did Gibbons' (1972) study of criminals in rural Oregon 30 years later. Dinitz (1973) conducted victimization research in a small Ohio town, representing one of the first attempts to use a crime or victimization survey in a rural locality. Furthermore, studies of rural juvenile delinquency by Lentz (1956), Feldhusen, Thurston, and Ager (1965) and Polk (1969) were early exceptions to the urban dominance of criminology. Further aggravating the situation was that those few early rural sociologists who examined rural crime did not cite very frequently the criminological literature, and vice versa, criminologists who paid any attention to rural crime did not integrate their research with the work of the rural sociologists. Hence, rural crime was mostly ignored, treated as a form of exceptionalism or as some sort of exotic curiosity by both disciplines, and exhibited little synergy or crossover between the intellectual traditions of rural sociology and criminology.

One event significantly changed the situation in the late 1970s and since then, rural crime scholarship has slowly but inexorably increased to the point that it is a vital area of scholarship, with research that varies by topic and approach. This was the founding of the National Rural Crime Prevention Center (NRCPC) at The Ohio State University by G. Howard Phillips, a rural sociologist (Carter, Phillips, Donnermeyer, & Wurschmidt, 1982). However, even though the research emanating from NRCPC was copious, it was descriptive and uncritical. Nonetheless, it influenced the development, for the first time, of a network of scholars who began to pursue sub-topics within rural crime that reflected many of the same themes found within criminology proper. In other words, at this point, researchers with rural interests began to talk to one another. Propelling rural criminology forward was publication of the first truly comprehensive review of the literature and overview of rural crime in *Crime and Policing in Rural and Small-Town America* by Weisheit et al. (2006), which is now in its third edition. This book brought rural crime to the attention of a great many scholars in criminology and criminal justice.

Yet, the conversation was without any kind of a critical perspective whereby rural crime was treated within the context of structural forms of inequality and a segmented social organization ripe with forms of patriarchy, racism, sexism, and worker exploitation. In fact, the first chapter of one of the more influential and recent works that have helped move rural criminology toward a more critical approach – *Crime and Conflict in the Countryside* (Dingwall & Moody, 1999) – soundly and justifiably pointed out the shortcomings of the earlier work of one of the authors (Donnermeyer, 1994) of this monograph:

> In particular, the work of the doyen of rural crime studies in America, Joseph F. Donnermeyer, provides a useful example of current research concerns ... he begins his analysis by noting that global factors – population mobility, urbanization, interdependence – shape crime trends in rural areas just as they do in urban areas. However, he soon leaves such abstractions behind, preferring to concentrate on a very broad statistical mapping exercise ... dinner with the Waltons may be filling and wholesome but *haute cuisine* it is not. Instead, this body of research appears to be politically naïve, methodologically simplistic and philosophically unengaged.
>
> *(Moody, 1999, pp. 14–15)*

One starting point for contemporary rural critical criminology, and still its strongest intellectual influence, is a feminist perspective about intimate partner violence in rural communities. Patricia Gagne's (1992, 1996) feminist work on rural woman abuse played an important part in sparking recent critical interpretations of crime and social control. Shortly after came Neil Websdale's (1998) *Rural Woman Battering and the Justice System: An Ethnography*, which also makes an important feminist contribution to a social scientific understanding of gender violence. Nonetheless, the flames did not emerge until the latter part of this decade with the publication of a flurry of scholarly materials, many of which continued along the feminist path broken by Gagne and Websdale (DeKeseredy & Donnermeyer, 2013). As well, among others, work by Kerry Carrington and associates (Carrington, 2007; Carrington & Scott, 2008; Carrington, Hogg, & McIntosh, 2011; Hogg & Carrington, 2006) on violent crime and masculinity in Australia, and by scholars such as Avi Brisman (South & Brisman, 2012) and Ken Tunnell at

Eastern Kentucky University (Tunnell, 2004, 2006; Donnermeyer & Tunnell, 2007) have helped build the intellectual infrastructure for a rural critical criminology.

Still, what all of the new directions in a critical rural criminology considered here have in common is that they take a different theoretical approach that is not beholden to or dependent on an urban-derived criminological theory unless it has some heuristic value. It is the utility of a theory, not its historical roots in a well-known school of criminology or the way that it enhances publication in mainstream criminology journals, that really counts. Prior to reviewing some recent rural critical criminological perspectives, it is first necessary to outline what we view as the key elements of a critical rural criminology.

Key elements of a critical rural criminology[5]

The key elements of a new or critical criminology called for by us nearly six years ago (see Donnermeyer & DeKeseredy, 2008) are similar to some of those recommended by Taylor, Walton, and Young (1973) four decades ago in their seminal *The New Criminology: For a Social Theory of Deviance*. Even so, this classic piece of critical scholarship was mainly a critique of orthodox theories (e.g., strain and social learning) and liberal perspectives, such as Becker's (1973) labeling theory (Matthews, 2003).[6] Further, Taylor et al.'s theoretical position was grounded primarily in a Marxian understanding of the political economy and how it shaped crime and societal reactions to it. According to them, crime is "a product of inequitable economic relationships in a context of general poverty" (p. 218).

While we and an international cadre of other critical criminologists (e.g., Reiner, 2012) agree that the capitalist political economic structure warrants careful consideration,[7] we contend that the patriarchal and ethnic relations that also control our society must be taken into account. Those familiar with the history of critical criminology are all too aware that Taylor et al.'s (1973) *The New Criminology* privileges economic conditions over gender, race/ethnicity, and culture (Matthews, 2003; Mooney, 2012). This is highly problematic because much of rural men's violence depends on an adherence to the ideology of familial patriarchy or their attempt to assert white hegemony, despite their class position

(Chakraborti & Garland, 2004; DeKeseredy & Schwartz, 2009; Perry, 2003). Thus, our call for what Taylor et al. (1973, p. 270) refer to as situating a criminal act "in terms of its wider structural origins" is broader in scope.

The wider origins of rural crime

In his commentary on Ireland, Thornberry, and Loeber's (2003) urban public housing violence research, Lab (2003) presents some arguments that are also used for a social scientific understanding of rural crime. For instance, he argues that:

> One of the most important things that criminologists often fail to address is the context in which they (their projects or topics) are operating. This is true whether they are proposing a new theory, testing an existing explanation, investigating an emerging phenomenon, or evaluating an intervention or program.

(p. 39)

As they progress through this new millennium, critical criminologists need to ask, "What is the broader social, political, and economic context in which crime is operating in rural parts of the world?" For rural North America, especially the U.S.A., this context is replete with environmental problems, poverty, and a decline of agriculture, timber, and mining jobs as machinery replaces labor (Freudenburg, 2006). Hurricanes Katrina and Isaac[8] and the BP oil spill added much to the ongoing pain and misery experienced by people who live in the northern Gulf of Mexico (DeKeseredy et al., 2013). More than 40% of black children in Louisiana, Mississippi, and Alabama live in poor families and more than 12% of people living in the first two of these three states have incomes that are less than half of the federal poverty level (Hotez, 2011; National Center for Children Living in Poverty, 2005). As well, the 12 million people living in the above states have the lowest incomes, lowest educational attainment, and the shortest life expectancy of people living in the U.S.A. (Burd-Sharps, Lewis, & Borges Martins, 2009). That the Gulf Coast states have the country's lowest human development score has "prompted a call by the American Human Development Project to launch a Marshall Plan for the Gulf, referring to a comprehensive reconstruction plan that resembles U.S. efforts to reconstruct Europe in the devastation that followed World War II" (Hotez, 2011, p. 1).

At the same time, throughout North America, there is a major decline in the number of family-owned farms because many people cannot make a reasonable living from them (DeKeseredy & Schwartz, 2009; Jacobs, 2005). Moreover, many rural towns, such as Nelsonville, Ohio, that had to rely on a few industries for employment, have been economically shattered by the closing of sawmills, coalmines, and other major sources of income.[9] Additionally, the "Wal-Marting" of the rural U.S.A. is forcing locally owned small businesses to shut down (Tunnell, 2006). Not only will this economic crisis increase involvement in rural drug trafficking, consumption, and production (see Chapter 3), but it will also exacerbate the problem of male-to-female violence in private places (DeKeseredy & Schwartz, 2009; Donnermeyer & DeKeseredy, 2008). As socialist feminists assert, class and gender relations are equally important, "inextricably intertwined," and "inseparable," and they interact to determine the social order at any particular time in history (Jaggar, 1983; Messerschmidt, 1986; Renzetti, 2012, 2013).

The social psychology of rural crime

The "formal requirement" of Taylor et al.'s (1973) new criminology involves explaining the different ways in which the aforementioned structural transitions "are interpreted, reacted against, or used by men at different levels in the social structure, in such as way that an essentially deviant choice is made" (p. 271). Presented in Figures 2.2 and 2.3 are theoretical models that respond to Taylor et al.'s concern and they are heavily influenced by some mainstream subcultural theorists (e.g., Cohen, 1955) who contend that socially and economically marginalized males create a collective or group solution to the problem of strain caused by challenges to their masculinity. Figures 2.2 and 2.3 are described later in this chapter and they include a key example (male peer support) of a "social psychological component" of a critical theory that addresses calls by Taylor et al. and other critical criminologists for focusing on "the precipitating causes of crime" (Matthews, 2003, p. 5).

A rural square of crime

The above two elements of a rural critical criminology exclude the role of the state, which is again becoming a central focus of much British critical criminological empirical, and theoretical work. Prime examples are Roger Matthews' (2009) refashioned left realism and Simon Hallsworth and John Lea's (2011) offering about a new state form that they label the "security state." It is worth noting, too, that a considerable amount of critical scholarship done in the 1970s and 1980s examined the role of the state and there were heated debates among Marxist scholars about this topic.[10] For the purpose of this book, following the late Marxist scholar Ralph Miliband (1969), the state consists of "the government, the administration, the police, the judicial branch, the subcentral government, and parliamentary assemblies" (p. 54).

How should a rural critical criminology address the role of the state? Perhaps one of the best answers to this question is found in British left realists' square of crime depicted in Figure 2.1. The square consists of four interacting elements: victim, offender, police and agencies of the state, and the public. Young (1992) describes the social relationships between each point on the square:

> It is the relationship between the police and the public which determines the efficacy of policing, the relationship between the victim and the offender which determines the impact of crime, the relationship between the state and the offender which is a major factor in recidivism.

(p. 27)

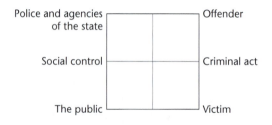

FIGURE 2.1 The square of crime.

The square of crime focuses simultaneously on criminal behavior or action and on societal, including state, reactions to it (Donnermeyer & DeKeseredy, 2008). Moreover, the square of crime shows that crime rates in many urban and rural communities are outcomes of four interrelated causes: (1) the causes of offending (e.g., unemployment and peer group membership); (2) factors that make victims vulnerable (e.g., lifestyles/routine activities); (3) the social conditions that influence public levels of control and tolerance; and (4) the social forces that propel agents of social control (e.g., police) (Young, 1992, p. 30).

Some readers might argue that since the square of crime is a dated contribution and that left realism has historically focused almost exclusively on inner-city street crime, it has little, if any, relevance to a critical criminological understanding of current criminal activities and social control in rural communities.[11] We fundamentally disagree with this notion and have recently offered a new left realist perspective on rural crime and societal reactions to it (see DeKeseredy & Donnermeyer, 2013). Furthermore, although Figures and 2.2 and 2.3 are strongly guided by feminist and male peer support theories of woman abuse in urban areas (DeKeseredy, Rogness, & Schwartz, 2004; DeKeseredy & Schwartz, 2002), they address key rural realities (e.g., loss of family farms) and are partially influenced by left realists' application of the concepts of strain and subculture to an understanding of crime. We reprise the square of crime for each of the three rural crime issues reviewed in Chapter 3 to illustrate the complexity of factors that must be considered if rural criminology is to take a conscious critical stance.

The call for a rural left realism is not new and dates back to a paper written by U.S. criminologist Darryl Wood (1990). He asserted that:

> Not only can left realism provide aid to the study of rural crime, but the study of rural crime can also support the foundations of left realism. That rural areas can also be impacted by working-class crime provides much to the left realist argument that the study of such behavior must go beyond the perspectives which have been fed to scholars for a long time now. And when we consider that the political economic situations of both inner-city citizens and rural citizens are

similar, left realism is provided with further justification for trying to provide a socialist response to working-class criminality.

(p. 14)

Yet, at the time of writing this book, no one has tested hypotheses derived from the square of crime in rural areas. We hope that someone will do so soon because the ever-expanding corpus of rural criminology is largely a-theoretical. And, we contend that the square of crime does not have an intrinsic urban bias, and instead, represents a way to understand the fundamental dimensions of crime at multiple levels. Feminism, too, strengthens a social scientific understanding of certain types of rural crime and two of the most widely cited rural critical criminological theories are partially shaped by feminist ways of knowing. They were co-authored by two North Americans who have publicly identified themselves as left realists for over 25 years and it is to their first rural theoretical contribution that we turn to next.

A feminist/male peer support model of separation and divorce sexual assault[12]

Walter DeKeseredy and Martin Schwartz are among a large group of critical criminologists who "wear two hats." In addition to publishing numerous articles and book chapters on left realism, they devote much time and effort to gathering qualitative and quantitative data on various types of woman abuse in intimate, heterosexual relationships. They have also spent close to 30 years theorizing the relationship between male peer support and woman abuse.[13] However, it was not until 2004 that they developed a critical theoretical framework that synthesizes current scholarship on "gendered violence and the architecture of rural life" (Hogg & Carrington, 2006, p. 171). Prior to taking on this task, the limited theoretical work that did exist on this topic ignored separation and divorce sexual assault. Of course, the neglect on the part of scholars to examine this variant of male-to-female violence applies to woman abuse research in general. To help fill the gap in the rural crime literature, together with their former Ohio University MA student McKenzie Rogness (see DeKeseredy et al., 2004), they constructed an empirically informed theory that allows for a simultaneous consideration of broader macro-level forces and micro-level gender relations of central concern to feminist scholars. Their theory presented in Figure 2.2 moves well beyond answering the problematic question, "Why doesn't she leave?" to "What happens when she leaves or tries to leave?" and "Why do men do it?" (Hardesty, 2002; Stark, 2007).[14]

Figure 2.2 situates separation/divorce sexual assault within the larger context of societal patriarchy. North America is a continent characterized by gross gender inequity. For instance, in 33 U.S. states, under law, a man can be awarded conditional exemptions if he rapes his wife (Caringella, 2009). Many more examples of patriarchal practices and discourses can easily be provided. Nevertheless, a constant such as societal patriarchy cannot explain a variable like changes in the frequency and severity of male sexual assaults on women who want to leave or have left them (Ellis & DeKeseredy, 1997). In other words, if we live in a patriarchal society that promotes male proprietariness, why, then, do some men sexually assault during or after the exiting process, whereas most do not? Certainly, data generated by a number of researchers using patriarchal ideology scales of one kind or another indicate that there are variations in male proprietariness (DeKeseredy et al., 2004; DeKeseredy & Schwartz, 1998; Smith, 1990), which is "the tendency [of men] to think of women as sexual and reproductive 'property' they can own and exchange" (Wilson & Daly, 1992, p. 85). Proprietariness refers to "not just the emotional force of [the male's] own feelings of entitlement but to a more pervasive attitude [of ownership and control] toward social relationships [with intimate female partners]" (p. 85).

Most women in abusive relationships or in nonviolent relationships characterized by other means of patriarchal dominance and control are not weak people who are unable to take steps on their own behalf. In fact, many women resist or eventually will resist their male partners' proprietariness in a variety of ways, such as arguing, protesting, and fighting back if they have been abused (DeKeseredy & Schwartz, 2013; Sev'er, 2002). For example, one southeast Ohio woman told DeKeseredy and Schwartz (2009): "With me being a strong-headed woman, I did not like that and I refused to cook for him, I refused to do his laundry. I told him to do it his damn self because I don't want to be his slave. He didn't like that. . . . That would usually have me end up with a fist in my face or my head bashed against a wall" (p. 41).

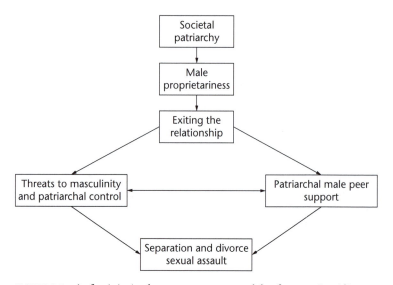

FIGURE 2.2 A feminist/male peer support model of separation/divorce sexual assault.

There are also women, although the precise number is unknown, who defy men's control by exiting or trying to exit a relationship and this may involve emotional separation, obtaining a separate residence, and/or starting or completing a legal separation/divorce. Emotional separation, a major predictor of a permanent end to a relationship, is defined as a woman's denial or restriction of sexual relations and other intimate exchanges (Ellis & DeKeseredy, 1997). Emotionally exiting a relationship can be just as dangerous as physically or legally exiting one because it, too, increases the likelihood of male violence and sexual abuse (Block & DeKeseredy, 2007; DeKeseredy & Schwartz, 2009; Kirkwood, 1993). For instance, of the 100 sexually abused women who participated in McFarlane and Malecha's (2005) study sponsored by the U.S. National Institute of Justice, 22% reported an emotional separation before the first time they were sexually assaulted.

Regardless of how a woman does it, her attempt to exit or her successful departure from a sexist relationship challenges male proprietariness, and may result in violence, including homicide (Dobash, Dobash,

Cavanagh, & Medina-Ariza, 2007; Websdale, 2010). As Lundy Bancroft (2002) states, "The abuser's dehumanizing view of his partner as a personal possession can grow even uglier as a relationship draws to a close" (p. 219). Nonetheless, exiting alone, like all single factors, cannot on its own account for sexual assault. For example, many abusive patriarchal men who abuse women during or after separation/divorce have male friends with similar beliefs and values, and these peers reinforce the notion that women's exiting is a threat to a man's masculinity (DeKeseredy et al., 2006). Moreover, many members of patriarchal peer groups view beatings, rapes, and other forms of male-to-female victimization as legitimate and effective means of repairing "damaged" patriarchal masculinity and reaffirming a man's right to control his female partner (Messerschmidt, 1993; Ray, 2011). Not only do these men verbally and publicly state that sexual assault and other forms of abuse are legitimate means of maintaining patriarchal authority and domination, they also serve as role models because many of them physically, sexually, and psychologically harm their own intimate partners. Consider that 47% of the 43 rural survivors of separation/divorce assault DeKeseredy and Schwartz (2009) talked to said that they knew their partners' friends also physically or sexually abused women. In fact, Betty, one of their respondents, told them that all of her ex-partner's friends hit women or sexually assaulted them, and several interviewees told us that they directly observed their partners' friends abusing female intimates.

In short, patriarchal male peer support contributes to the perception of damaged masculinity and motivates sexually abusive men to "lash out against the women … they can no longer control" (Bourgois, 1995, p. 214). Moreover, if a patriarchal man's peers see him as a failure with women because his partner wants to leave or has left him, he is likely to be ridiculed because he "can't control his woman" (DeKeseredy et al., 2004). Hence, like many college men who rape women, he is likely to sexually assault her to regain status among his peers. Similar to other men who rape female strangers, acquaintances or dates, the sexual assaults committed by men during or after the process of separation/divorce may have much more to do with their need to sustain their status among their peers than either a need to satisfy their sexual desires or a longing to regain a loving relationship (Godenzi, Schwartz, & DeKeseredy, 2001).

Figure 2.2 guided DeKeseredy and Schwartz's (2009) study of separation/divorce sexual assault in rural Ohio and it garnered some empirical support. Still, there are obviously other factors that contribute to separation/divorce assaults, such as male consumption of pornography (DeKeseredy, in press; DeKeseredy & Olsson, 2011; DeKeseredy & Schwartz, 2009). As well, Figure 2.2 served as a launching pad for future theoretical work and the next section features a subsequent perspective that addresses some major rural issues that were overlooked at the time of its development.

A rural masculinity crisis/male peer support model of separation/divorce assault[15]

Nearly 10 years ago, a fortuitous meeting took place at Moretti's of Arlington. This is an Italian restaurant in Columbus, Ohio, located close to The Ohio State University (OSU). OSU sociologist Ruth Peterson was then Director of the school's Criminal Justice Research Center (CJRC) and she invited Walter DeKeseredy to make a presentation on the preliminary results of his rural Ohio separation/divorce sexual assault study at the Center.[16] Walter was taken out to dinner at Moretti's the night before and there he met Joseph (Joe) Donnermeyer, the co-author of this book. Walter was then a neophyte in rural crime research, but had a long history of doing critical criminological work, especially feminist research and theorizing. Joe, on the other hand, had vast experience doing the former, but relatively little doing the latter, as noted so vividly by Moody's (1999) critique. Still, we had many common interests, including a deep-rooted commitment to studying the plight of rural people and to struggling for social justice. Walter continues to tell friends and colleagues that Joe was always a critical criminologist but did not know it.[17]

Several years later, Walter asked Joe to help him and three other colleagues develop the theoretical model presented in Figure 2.3 (DeKeseredy et al., 2007). Joe eagerly accepted the invitation and a strong friendship and intellectual partnership soon emerged. Of course, no adequate perspective on the relationship between male peer support and woman abuse, regardless where this crime takes place, is complete without the input of Martin Schwartz. He contributed much to the

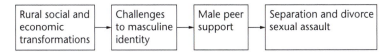

FIGURE 2.3 A rural masculinity crisis/male peer support model of separation/divorce sexual assault.

project, along with Eastern Kentucky University criminologist Kenneth Tunnell and University of Hawaii PhD student Mandy Hall, who was one of Walter's former MA students.

Rural social and economic transformations, challenges to masculine identity, and male peer support are major components of Figure 2.3. Following Sernau (2006), this model asserts that in rural U.S. communities, "male privilege is persistent but precarious" (p. 69). For example, prior to the end of the 20th century, many rural men obtained an income from owning family farms or working in extractive industries such as coal mining (Jensen, 2006; Lobao & Meyer, 2001; Sherman, 2005). Further, buttressed by a patriarchal ideology, most of these men's marriages were typically characterized by a rigid gendered division of labor in which men were the primary "bread winners" and women had "an intense and highly privatized relationship with domestic production," such as childrearing and doing housework (Websdale, 1998, p. 49; see also Ni Laoire & Fielding, 2006). This is not to say, though, that such gender relations are non-existent today. They are still evident in a sizeable number of rural communities (Lobao, 2006). Reflect on the experiences of this rural Ohio woman interviewed by DeKeseredy & Schwartz (2009):

> His favorite thing was, "If you are not going to be at work, you're going to be here cooking and cleaning, doing laundry. And if I ever catch you sitting on your ass, I am going to beat the fuck out of you, you know."
>
> *(p. 71)*

Even so, rural men's power has become fragile due to major challenges to their masculine identity spawned by changes that have occurred over the last 40 or more years (DeKeseredy et al., 2007; Johnson, 2006;

Sherman, 2005). For example, there is a major decline in the number of family-owned farms because many people cannot make a reasonable living from them (Jacobs, 2005; Toews, 2010). Furthermore, the closing of sawmills, coal mines, and other key sources of income have devastated many rural U.S. communities that relied on a small number of industries for employment (Jensen, 2006; United States Department of Agriculture, 2011). Also, many women seek employment or get jobs when their husbands become unemployed or when their farms become unsustainable or less profitable – another factor that has the potential for weakening the overall power of men (DeKeseredy & Schwartz, 2009; Lobao & Meyer, 2001). As Gallup-Black (2005) correctly observed when considering the vast literature on the linkage between disadvantage and homicide in urban locations, "But the relationship between violence and economic hardship … defined by job loss, unemployment, poverty, and population loss – can be just as pronounced in rural or small population areas" (p. 165). Recall the rural violence data presented in Chapter 1.

This transition in the area of employment often generates marital instability because many economically displaced males who cannot meet their perceived responsibilities as the man of the household feel deprived of intimate and social support resources that give them self-worth (DeKeseredy & Schwartz, 2009). A sizeable portion of unemployed rural men who strongly adhere to the ideology of familial patriarchy compensate for their lack of economic power by exerting more control over their wives (DeKeseredy et al., 2007; Sherman, 2005), a problem that can influence these women to consider leaving or to exit their marriages. Numerous other major social and economic transitions have spawned "the crisis in the rural gender order" (Hogg & Carrington, 2006, p. 181), such as women's rights to own property and inherit wealth, an increase in the number of rural women's associations, and the "delegitimation" of some forms of rural masculinity (e.g., via tougher drinking and driving laws).

Some unemployed rural men have "managed to remake masculinity" (Sherman, 2005, p. 6) through means that do not involve intense patriarchal domination and control of their wives or common-law partners. For instance, Sherman's (2005) study of families harmed by the closure of sawmills in a rural California community reveals that some unemployed men became active, progressive fathers and delighted in spending much time with their children while their wives worked. Too many other unemployed rural men, however, deal with the aforementioned "masculinity challenges" by spending much time drinking with men in similar situations (DeKeseredy et al., 2006), which is one of the key reasons why their wives leave or try to leave them (Sherman, 2005). Frequently, the contexts of drinking, such as bars and pubs, are locations where definitions of masculinity are played out (Campbell, 2006), what Campbell (2000) referred to as the "glass phallus." Further, as DeKeseredy and Schwartz (2009) uncovered in three rural Ohio counties, many rural men have peers who view various types of woman abuse as legitimate and effective means of repairing damaged masculinity. Similar to many unemployed urban counterparts, these men serve as abusive role models (DeKeseredy & Schwartz, 2013).

When women terminate relationships because of their partners' substance abuse, violent behavior, or other problems generated in part by unemployment, rural men often perceive this move as another threat to their masculinity. Additionally, many of them are influenced by their male peers to engage in separation/divorce sexual assault to regain control and to avoid losing status (DeKeseredy et al., 2007). Status is a factor that is also closely related to fear of ridicule, which is a mechanism of informal social control in many societies (Bierstedt, 1957; Warr, 2002). For example, if abusive men's peers see them as failures with women due to separation/divorce, they will face group ridicule, lose status, and thus assault the women they can no longer dominate (Bourgois, 1995). This process is similar to the dynamics behind the presentation of self by males in rural pubs, as described by Campbell (2000). It is not so much demonstrating masculinity as it is being seen by peers as less than masculine. Hence, control and abuse prevent loss of status.

Unlike mainstream theories which inform rural criminology, Figure 2.3 does not reduce gender to an afterthought. It is a rare attempt to examine the plight of a group of women who have historically suffered in silence. Indeed, if battered lesbians, women of color, and female members of other ethnic/racial groups have been delegated to the margins by orthodox criminology (Sokoloff & Dupont, 2005), the same can be said about socially and economically excluded rural women who endure the harms identified here.

We argue for expanding a critical perspective of rural criminology beyond the borders of Australia, Canada, Great Britain and the U.S.A., where most previous rural work has been produced. For example, there is some published research on violence against rural women in countries like India, which has been in the news recently for several sensationalized cases of gang rape (see Chapter 3). Even though they occurred in cities, there are Indian scholars who have focused their scholarly lens on the plight of rural women in India (Bhattacharyya, Bedi, & Chhachhi, 2011; Krishnan, 2005; Panda & Agarwal, 2005; Scrinivasan & Bedi, 2007). Further, research on violence against rural women in Africa (Jewkes et al., 2006; Leach, 2006) reminds us that nearly half of the world is rural. Across the diversity of these rural places comes the full gamut of crime issues – from violent and property crime to environmental crime and human trafficking – to be examined.

Summary

When rural crime, as an established sub-field within criminology, began its development in the last quarter of the 20th century (Carter et al., 1982), much of the research was descriptive and a-theoretical. Gradually, this situation has changed. Yet the simultaneous advancement of theory and research devoted to crime in the rural context remains uneven. Most of the emphasis is on place-based theories, which is understandable given the obvious geographic aspects of rural and remote areas, but many other possibly useful theories have been ignored, especially critical perspectives such as those reviewed in this chapter on research related to violence against rural women.

Rural crimes and societal reactions to them are attracting the attention of a growing number of criminologists around the world. As well, the qualitative and quantitative studies done on these topics, for the most part, meet the highest disciplinary standards and the results of these projects are published in top-ranked journals of criminology and sociology, such as the *British Journal of Criminology* (e.g., Carrington & Scott, 2008; Walters, 2004, 2006), *Criminology* (e.g., Lee, 2008; Osgood & Chambers, 2000), *Sociologia Ruralis* (Jobes, Donnermeyer & Barclay, 2005), and *Violence Against Women* (e.g., DeKeseredy & Joseph, 2006; Rennison et al., in press). Nonetheless, theoretical developments have not kept pace with the burgeoning empirical literature on crime, law, and social control in rural places. Furthermore, the bulk of the theoretical work done so far is mainly orthodox, and ecological perspectives, such as social disorganization theory, are the dominant schools of thought despite consistently being the targets of sharp criticism. For example, Matthew R. Lee (2008) asserts that:

> existing ecologically based theories, such as the social disorganization model, rely on a very narrow conception of the appropriate unit of analysis – neighborhoods – for the theoretical processes specified in the model. This analysis is extremely problematic for the rural context given that conventional urban-type neighborhoods are few and far between and that in many places the nearest neighbors actually live miles apart.
>
> *(p. 468)*

If theories such as the social disorganization perspective are so problematic, why, then, do they continue to be applied and discussed? If it is, as Donnermeyer (2012) notes in his review of the critical criminological literature on rural crime, "time to make Tönnies and Wirth go away!" (p. 290), maybe it is also time to make functionalist renditions of ecological perspectives go away. Regardless, though, of whether these models stay or go, it is time to take theorizing rural crime to a higher level, one that integrates macro- and micro-levels of analysis. The critical criminological perspectives reviewed here certainly do that. They are starting points in the development of new ways of understanding social problems but more elements of a new or critical rural criminology still need to be fleshed out. We hope that more rural sociologists and criminologists will examine the interrelations among broader social, economic, and political forces and crime, as well as societal reactions to violations of law. On top of what Lee and others say about place-based theories, the failure to consider these wider influences is one of the most significant problems with applications of models derived from the Chicago School and the New Chicago School (Donnermeyer & DeKeseredy, 2008).

A new or rural critical criminology cannot afford to be stagnant and the theoretical models presented in Figures 2.1, 2.2, and 2.3 are the beginnings for future theoretical work. Subsequent offerings need to address some important rural realities conspicuously absent from these models. For example, they focus mainly on acts of interpersonal violence. To be sure, more theoretical work on this topic is warmly welcomed, but there is also a major need to construct critical theories in other areas. In the next chapter, we use the square of crime as one of many possible critical perspectives to re-examine three areas where a great deal of rural work has already been accomplished, namely, communities and rural crime, drugs use, production and trafficking, and agricultural crime.

3

CREATING THE CRITICAL IN RURAL CRIMINOLOGY

> But numbers are signs to be interpreted within specific cultural contexts, figures in themselves do not have any magical objectivity. In this way the balance between numbers and conceptualization shifts, instead of numbers dominating and concepts atrophying, theory and conceptualization take centre stage and numbers find their place, wherever appropriate, fully situated and contextualized. It is not more and fancier statistical testing that will solve the problems of numbers in the social sciences, rather it is theory and conceptualization ... that will give numbers relevance, utility and their place.
>
> *(Young, 2011, p. 55)*

In the first two chapters, we showed how rural criminology has blossomed in recent times but lamented the field's general lack of a critical perspective. Through our review of research on violence against rural women, we demonstrated how a critical approach adds new insights, great scholarly value, and high potential for the future development of a more comprehensive version of a critical rural criminology. In this chapter we continue our quest by examining the rural-focused literature in three areas: (1) communities and crime; (2) substance use and drug production/trafficking; and (3) agricultural crime.

We selected these three areas because there is a sufficient corpus of work in each which is ripe for reanalysis from a critical point of view. First, the current body of work on the rural community and crime is already moving toward a more critical consideration of social control within a localized context, and holds great promise for challenging many mainstream criminological theories and concepts (i.e., a non-functionalist ecology). Second, research on drug use among rural populations and drug production in rural areas adds additional support to dispelling the four myths about rural crime which we addressed in Chapter 1 (Young, 1992; Donnermeyer & DeKeseredy, 2008). Finally, a relatively smaller body of largely a-theoretical, empirical work on agricultural crime is reframed within a critical framework, and by doing so, we demonstrate the potential for examining how food production and food producers fit within the larger social structural and social class contexts of their societies, including a view of agriculturalists as both the victims of crime and individuals who can commit serious violations of the law.

For each topic, we use the square of crime to help summarize the extant literature and where it fits in a critical interpretation. We do not claim that the square of crime provides the most comprehensive, or even the most heuristic, perspective for each topic. However, we adopt it to show how a consistently applied critical framework can help move a largely a-theoretical base of research forward toward a more critical form of rural criminology.

The rural community and crime

Perhaps no criminological theory is more responsible for its urban-centric bias than social disorganization theory (Donnermeyer, 2007b).[1] Yet, no theory is more often adopted for empirical tests of the association of community characteristics and rural crime than social disorganization. And, ironically, no theory has helped shape a collective body of scholarship which has now laid the foundation for both a critical criminological view of community and rural crime, and a critique of a dominant strand of mainstream criminological thought, especially in the United States, which is today best known by the moniker "collective efficacy" (Sampson, 2012). Indeed, there is a Hegelian (Russell, 1945) flavor to this observation, but not in the normal sequence of stages, for the relationship of rural criminology and social disorganization theory is more like antithesis, synthesis, and thesis. In other words, as we observed in Chapter 1, an exposé of the sleigh-of-hand myth that collective efficacy equals low crime such that rural is unimportant to the criminological enterprise (*antithesis*)[2] can be found in the accumulated and summarized findings (*synthesis*) of largely quantitative rural community studies, non-critical in approach, which call into question the generalizability of this equation, and allow for the development of a very straightforward, but critical *thesis*. It is this: *there is no such thing as social disorganization, there are only forms of social organization which concurrently (within the same space or ecology) shape what is considered criminal and what is not, and how much various types of criminal behaviors are tolerated, condoned, condemned, and enforced.*

Place has always been a prominent feature of criminological thought. Called by a variety of names – community, neighborhood, city, town, shire, county, township, and village – the ecology of crime can even be seen in the nearly two-century-old scholarship of Rawson (1839), who compared crime across diverse places in England and Wales. His working premise was that neither climate nor the "race" composition of people could explain differing levels of crime in various places in England and Wales, so instead he examined, along with gender and age, whether places with dominant forms of industry and employment – agriculture, mining, manufacturing, and diverse, large, metropolitan communities – would display differences in the occurrence of crime. Indeed, they did, and to quote Sampson (2012, p. 33): "He found a low incidence of crime in the small mining counties and the mountainous districts of Northern England and Wales, and no differences in the crime rates between manufacturing and agricultural counties." No mention, however, does Sampson (2012) make of Rawson's (1839) detailed discussion of measurement problems in which he concluded that "It has already been shown that the official tables ... cannot in any way be used as evidence of the actual amount of crime committed or detected in the country" (p. 337).

Social disorganization is a theory which emphasizes variations in the social structure of places, and starts with the fundamental assumption that places with high levels of cohesion and solidarity have lower rates of crime, while places with less order and more disorganization display more crime (Kubrin, 2009; Sampson, 2012). The theory is an attempt to show that locality, especially neighborhoods within urban places, affects crime beyond the demographic composition of its residents. In essence, it harkens back to Émile Durkheim's (1965) description of social facts as *sui generis*. As Kubrin (2009, p. 227) sums it up: "What social disorganization theory has to offer then is a specification of the effects of neighborhood characteristics on the capacity and ability of community residents to implement and maintain public norms."

But, as both Merton (1949) and Gans (1972) asked many decades ago, for whom are the public norms to which Kubrin (2009) refers dysfunctional, and for whom are they functional?[3] Hence, one can imagine a way for social disorganization theory to engage in a more critical form of scholarship about crime, but that certainly has not been the case with the theory up to now. From Shaw and McKay (1942) to Sampson (2012), there is a continuous fallback to the notion of a dichotomy reminiscent of the way the earlier *Gemeinschaft–Gesellschaft* distinction of Tönnies was misinterpreted, as well as a host of other dichotomies and typological continuums which were used to explain the transformation of societies from rural and agrarian to urban and industrial (McKinney, 1966). Simply put, the dichotomy says that crime must be due to disorder, lack of cohesion, lower levels of collective efficacy – conditions of the city, not the countryside (Donnermeyer, 2007b, 2012) – hence, antithesis. Significant variation and diversity of social organization are largely between neighborhoods and communities, and mostly not within.

Despite the emphasis on social structural properties, which is more than the sum of the characteristics of individuals residing at places, much of the research based on social disorganization theory deals only with the antecedents of social structure, such as residential instability (i.e., the proportion of residents who have moved in recently), the race/ethnic heterogeneity of the population, and economic measures such as employment rates and poverty levels (Bursik, 1988). As well, only a small part of the literature uses anything other than official statistics, such as crimes reported to the police or arrest rates, data that even Rawson in 1839 knew were inadequate (Warner & Pierce, 1993; Kaylen & Pridemore, 2011).

Fortunately, recent attempts adhere more closely to the original idea behind the theory, which is to measure informal social control as a condition of localized social structure. Hence, the work of Bursik (1988, 1999), Sampson (2012), and others have morphed social disorganization into a series of concepts, the most popular of which is "collective efficacy," but including other well-known variants, such as cohesion, integration, civility or civic community/society, density of acquaintanceship, and social capital. Admittedly, each has its own distinctive meaning, but together they form a tightly knit cluster of concepts with similar connotations, like a set of overlapping Venn diagrams.

As was the case with Rawson, some of the first attempts to examine crime in the rural context during the first half of the 20th century were place-based or ecological in perspective, but descriptive, such as Wood's (1942) analysis of the relationship of crime to the social organization of small towns in Wisconsin, Useem and Waldner's (1942) examination of crime patterns in a rural South Dakota county, and Lagey's (1957) consideration of the ecology of juvenile delinquency in a rural area of Pennsylvania. Research such as Clark and Wenninger's (1962) comparative study of social class, community size, and delinquency (half of the sample was from Chicago) and Dinitz's (1973) examination of small-town life and crime in western Ohio were likewise place-based, but did not embrace social disorganization or any other kind of criminological theory. Even though all five studies were pioneers in the development of rural criminology, each was simply interested in ecological variations as a type of early epidemiological analysis of crime in rural localities.

Eventually, as rural criminology's body of scholarship began to gradually expand, social disorganization theory and other closely associated variants were some of the first to be adopted for application to the study of crime in the rural context (Donnermeyer et al., 2006; Donnermeyer, 2007). However, before we review and critically reinterpret these, we need to acknowledge predecessors whose research focus and findings were place-based, even though they did not embrace social disorganization theory.

The precursor studies within rural criminology that examined communities and rural crime but did not use social disorganization theory come in three variants. First, in the spirit of Wirth (1938), a series of similar (to some extent) studies by Fischer (1980, 1995), Laub (1983), Tittle (1989), Ingram (1993), Nolan (2004), and Rotolo and Tittle (2006) asked questions about variations of crime with levels of urbanization and urbanism. Urbanization refers to population size and population density, while urbanism refers to factors such as tolerance for differences, anomie, weaker social bonds, and lessened social control, all of which are presumed to be more characteristic of city life (Ingram, 1993). Although this subset of research is firmly rooted in the traditions of the Chicago School of sociology, and even though the authors cite many of the scholars most linked with the classic expressions of social disorganization theory, they do not explicitly use the theory to examine the relationship of social structure and crime. As well, although not rural focused, or for that matter, manifestly centered on place-based factors other than population size and race/ethnicity and other variables for the purposes of statistical control, these studies at least recognized that location is more than the aggregated characteristics of its inhabitants. Further, even though these criminologists mostly found a positive relationship between size of place and crime, it was not a simple, "monotonic," and "linear" association. Even though their study ignored places with fewer than 25,000 persons, Rotolo and Tittle (2006) concluded that "It may be inaccurate to claim that city size is monotonically related to crime rates or to assume that increases or decreases in population may portend corresponding increases or decreases in crime rates" (p. 359). Their parting statement is most interesting: "Current urban theory does not even fully anticipate or explain our findings, much less anticipating and explaining more complicated possibilities" (p. 360).

Second, there is a substantial body of work on the economic and social correlates of rural homicide and cultures of violence (Bankston and Allen, 1980; Berthelot, Blanchard, & Brown, 2008; Kowalski & Duffield, 1990; Lee, 2008; Lee & Stevenson, 2006; Nelsen et al., 1994; Nisbett, 1993; Petee & Kowalski, 1993; Wilkinson, 1984a; 1984b; Wilkinson, Reynolds, Thompson, & Ostresh, 1984). Also, there are number of published research studies that more generally attempt to correlate rural and economic development with crime (Arthur, 1991; Lee, 2006; Lee & Bartkowski, 2004a; 2004b; Lee, Maume, & Ousey, 2003; Lee & Ousey, 2001; Lee & Slack, 2008; Rephann, 1999). All of this research explicitly considers variations in crime by place; however, the unit of analysis is mostly the metropolitan–non-metropolitan status of a U.S. county, or clusters of counties within larger regions. Some of these analyses are explicitly rural, while others subsume rural and urban within a measure of a county's size of place (i.e., urbanization), which in turn is one variable in a larger, multivariate analysis of homicide, violence, and crime in general.

Third, a spate of articles about rural communities in the western region of the U.S.A. considered the disruptive effects of energy and natural resource development in terms of the effects of rapid growth on crime and fear of crime (Freudenburg & Jones, 1991; Krannich, Berry, & Greider, 1989; Krannich, Greider, & Little, 1985; Wilkinson, Thompson, Reynolds, & Ostresh, 1982; Wilkinson et al., 1984). Like most community-based research, both rural and urban, which utilizes social disorganization theory, these studies considered the effects of change on specific localities, and saw change as disruptive of an established social order. In general, the studies were quantitative in orientation, using surveys, official statistics, and occasionally delved into the qualitative side by collecting data from key informants. They found that development causes crime to increase at a rate greater than any population increase associated with the development (Freudenburg & Jones, 1991), and that concern and fear about crime increases as well (Krannich et al., 1989). However, they largely failed to interpret their findings from a more critical perspective, which would have seen these changes as a modification of the social organization of the local community with new arrangements due to external forces, with differential consequences for the local populace based on social class and other forms of inequality.

Today, the theme of rapid change from natural resource and energy development efforts has been taken up by Carrington and associates in rural Australia, but from a more critical point of view (Carrington, McIntosh, & Scott, 2010; Carrington et al., 2011; Carrington, McIntosh, Hogg, & Scott, 2013). These studies have honed in on how the changing social organization and cultural context of Australia's rural communities, both agriculture- and mining-dependent, affect men's identities, which in turn, influences expressions of violence, including forms of domestic abuse. Hence, they ask explicitly critical questions – functional for whom/dysfunctional for whom? – about resource development by examining, close up, diversity and change as expressed in the contexts of specific places.

The first explicit adoption of social disorganization theory to the study of communities and rural crime was an article published in *Rural Sociology* in 1993 on how off-shore oil development impacts rural parishes (equivalent to a county) in the state of Louisiana (Seydlitz, Laska, Spain, Triche,

& Bishop, 1993). Hence, it can also be considered in the cluster of scholarly work described above. The authors describe social disorganization theory in a way similar to Kubrin's (2009) summative statement:

> The theory proposes that massive immigration, which accompanies rapid industrialization, increases population density, which elevates suspicion, anonymity and competition for resources; reduces concern for neighbors and surveillance; contributes to poorer social relationships and poorer childcare; increases the independence of individuals; and impedes informal social control.
>
> *(Seydlitz et al., 1993 p. 97)*

Aside from the Armageddon-like tone of their statement, they address an issue also considered by Sampson (2012). One criticism of social disorganization theory is that, by using demographic and other aggregated characteristics (usually, some form of census data) of populations within places as proxies for internal features of control and cohesion (i.e., collective efficacy), researchers have failed to conduct a full, empirical test of the theory (Kaylen & Pridemore, 2012). Interestingly, Seydlitz et al. (1993) also adopted what they termed "relative deprivation" theory, which they defined as considering the localized effects of economic inequality, to their analysis in order to supplement social disorganization theory, in part because they were not completely confident that the theory was appropriate for the "boomtown" phenomena. Yet, they also failed to measure factors that Bursik (1988, 1999) would argue are necessary to understand the "systemic" nature of formal and informal controls within communities on crime. However, the authors do conclude that suicide and homicide rates go up during periods of activity in parishes more highly dependent on the oil industry, but that the rate of suicide and homicide is no different between more oil dependent and less oil dependent parishes.

The Seydlitz et al. (1993) article was the beginning of a steady parade of published studies of rural communities and crime utilizing social disorganization theory (Donnermeyer, Barclay, & Jobes, in press; Barnett & Mencken, 2002; Bouffard & Muftić, 2006; Cancino, 2005; Ceccato & Dolmen, 2011; Deller & Deller, 2010; Donnermeyer, Jobes, & Barclay, 2006, 2009; Jobes, 1999; Jobes et al., 2004, 2005; Kaylen, 2010;

Kaylen & Pridemore, 2011, 2012, 2013; Lee, 2006, 2008; Lee & Bartkowski, 2004a; 2004b; Lee & Ousey, 2001; Lee et al., 2003; Lee & Thomas, 2010; Li 2012; Mencken & Barnett, 1999; Osgood & Chambers, 2000; Ousey & Lee, 2010; Resig & Cancino, 2004; Spano & Nagy, 2005; Tunnell, 2006; Wells & Weisheit, 2004, 2012).[4] To a great extent, this body of work was uniform (or shall we say cohesive) in mostly focusing on the traditionally cited antecedents of social disorganization (residential instability, ethnic/race heterogeneity, family instability, etc.), or testing mediating influences of a neighborhood's social and cultural context on crime as measured by official police statistics (crimes known to the police and/or arrest and conviction data).

To highlight a few, Mencken and Barnett (1999) discovered no "spatial autocorrelation" effects in an analysis of homicide in the mid-south region of the U.S.A. using various measures derived from social disorganization theory. In more pedestrian nomenclature, what they found was that their unit of analysis, the county, was viable for measuring place-based social and economic indicators with crime. If they had found otherwise, most of the rural community and crime research might have to be thrown out because so much of it relies on county or county equivalent level measures (as indicators of neighborhood-like characteristics) to spin their statistics and their interpretations. As well, if spatial auto-correlation is a problem for a rural community analysis of crime, it would portend even greater difficulties for studies that consider inter-neighborhood differences when they are clustered in the same metropolitan area and are contiguous to other neighborhoods in the analysis, such as in Chicago. Later studies by Kaylen (2010) and Kaylen and Pridemore (2011, 2012) also tested for problems of spatial auto-correlation as a possible explanation for differences in results between rural and urban-located studies which adopted social disorganization theory. Their results also indicated no real problems that would call into question the validity of their research findings, or those of other researchers who adopt the social disorganization framework.

Perhaps the most frequently cited rural-focused article utilizing social disorganization theory is Osgood and Chamber's (2000) attempt to explain variations in rural youth violence. They noted a distinctive feature of non-metropolitan counties (their unit of analysis) from metropolitan counties, namely, that poverty and population mobility were negatively correlated in rural communities, whereas the direction of the relationship was positive in the urban setting. Hence, these two commonly accepted features of social disorganization theory did not go hand-in-hand in the rural context, which was why Osgood and Chambers (2000) did not find an association between poverty and arrest rates for violence offenses by youth. Other rural-focused research has found this same distinctive pattern (Bouffard & Muftić, 2006; Jobes et al., 2004; Kaylen & Pridemore, 2013; Wells & Weisheit, 2012), which is that economic indicators are less strong in predicting variations in crime within rural communities. Hence, the significance of the Osgood and Chambers (2000) article is that it was the first in a series of research studies which pointed toward two key weaknesses or limitations to social disorganization theory, and toward a greater complexity at places than the theory can account for. In other words, simple, "monotonic" relationships are not supportable when put to a statistical test; hence, rural results put a general strain on mainstream criminological theories like social disorganization.

Since all of the articles cited use official arrest data, it is possible that there is not only a different pattern in the relationship of poverty and crime within rural localities, but that on the other side of those ubiquitous multivariate equations, perhaps the issue is the dependent variable as well. It is quite possible that high poverty rural communities with low population mobility have a social or moral order which keeps violence, both intimate partner violence (DeKeseredy & Schwartz, 2009) and other forms of violence as well, in the dark (Barclay et al., 2004; Carrington et al., 2011). Hence, reporting violence is suppressed, which is functional for a hegemonic, patriarchal moral order for the offenders, but not so functional for the victims. Even if it is not suppressed, perhaps particular kinds of rural communities simply have a higher tolerance than urban residents for violence, hence, supporting to some extent earlier work on the regional culture of violence, which had decided rural overtones (Nelsen et al., 1994; Nisbett, 1993). Finally, poor rural communities may have fewer police resources and the police there may be less willing to recognize certain forms of violence as criminal (Weisheit et al., 2006).

Lee and associates have extended the analysis of rural communities and crime by re-examining the issue using the concept of "civic community" (Lee, 2006, 2008; Lee & Thomas, 2010; Ousey & Lee, 2010). The sequence of their analyses shows an interesting turn in their interpretation. First off, as described by Wells and Weisheit (2012), civic community theory, although similar to social disorganization, does not derive from a criminological base. Instead, it has developed out of the literature on social capital and community development. Yet, it is similar to social disorganization theory because it assumes that high levels of engagement by citizens in a community indicate greater solidarity and cohesion, hence, less crime. Lee and associates pioneered the application of this theory to the rural context. As first, they found substantial support for the civic community hypothesis. For example, rural counties with high per capita church membership had lower rates of violent crime (Lee, 2006). Extending his rural analysis, Lee (2008) also found that a stable population (a traditional exogenous factor in social disorganization theory) more likely led to a community where citizens displayed a greater investment, for example through membership in local, civic groups, voting, and church membership, which in turn was associated with lower rates of violent crime. And, indeed, that is what he found, even after controlling for economic factors. Lee and Thomas (2010) refined their analysis but found essentially the same thing, which was that a stable population enhanced residents' engagement in their community, which in turn reduced overall rates of violent crime, as measured by official statistics.

However, in the same year as the Lee and Thomas (2010) article, Ousey and Lee (2010) published results from a study which is curiously reminiscent of Merton's (1949) and Gans' (1972) observations about functionality. Considering the "dark side" of social capital, they conducted an analysis of the extent to which a highly engaged or civic community creates greater racial differences in rates of arrests for violent crime, as well as the alternative possibility that a highly engaged community reduced racial inequality. These results were mixed, indicating partial support for both sides of the issue. As the title of their article ("Whose Civic Community?") suggests, there is more to collective efficacy than a simple assumption that it is uniform across a neighborhood or town, and that it is inversely associated with all forms of crime.

Further confounding the civic community approach were the results of a national-level analysis of non-metropolitan counties by Wells and

Weisheit (2012). They conducted a comparative statistical analysis of violent and property crime rates for nearly 3,000 counties in the United States, using sets of independent variables traditionally adopted for testing social disorganization theory (population instability, racial heterogeneity, poverty, and family instability) plus civic community theory (owner-occupied housing, church membership, voting rates). The social disorganization variables were better predictors than the civic community factors across all four types of counties, which included metropolitan counties (counties with a city of ≥50,000) and three kinds of non-metropolitan counties based on the size of their largest city or town, but none with a place larger than 50,000 persons. Even so, the civic community model did explain some of the variance after controlling for the effects of the social disorganization derived variables. However, more importantly, the ability of either theory to explain either crimes rates or arrest rates diminished by rurality. Simply put, the theories were less than generalizable beyond the concentric circles of cities and suburbs.

Likewise, Kaylen and Pridemore (2011, 2012, 2013) have conducted an extensive re-evaluation of social disorganization theory and a point-by-point response to the earlier published article by Osgood and Chambers (2000), because its appearance in *Criminology* (which Osgood now edits) makes it the most frequently cited article on the relationship of rural community characteristics and crime. They tried using alternative dependent variables (such as hospital admissions for assault) and switched over their analysis from U.S. sources of data to the British Crime Survey (mimicking previous research by Sampson and Groves [1989]) to measure a full model of social disorganization, not simply the antecedents. They also checked for the possibility of auto-correlation, similar to Mencken and Barnett (1999). Their journey through the nuances of social disorganization theory is a remarkable story of rigorous scholarship, even though their scholarship leans heavily on quantitative analysis and a non-critical approach to the subject matter. Indeed, their accumulated results demonstrate, as the quote from Young's *The Criminological Imagination* (2011) at the beginning of this chapter advised, that numbers can be significant if considered within the framework of theory. And, their bottom line was this: "The most consistent finding, thus far, is a lack of support for the generalizability of the theory, as it has been tested, to rural communities" (Kaylen & Pridemore, 2012, p. 148).

So, a couple of dozen studies of crime rate variations in rural communities using either social disorganization theory or closely allied models and concepts have now been completed, and in almost every case these studies have hurled an arsenal of control and independent variables at a number of moving targets known as dependent variables, launched by a variety of multivariate statistical platforms, and the results all seem to point toward the limited utility of the very framework most closely associated with the Chicago School of sociology. Many critical criminologists, that is, many of this book's readers, probably cannot resist a know-it-all smirk, thinking to themselves that of course the theory is useless, as it is the end result of outmoded functionalist thinking (minus a couple tidbits of wisdom by Merton and Gans) and way too much abstracted empiricism. And, how ironic! A theory that eschewed the importance of the rural (*antithesis*), after an array of robust statistical studies (*synthesis*), can now be "put out to pasture" (to use an agricultural metaphor).

We propose instead to move forward by expanding upon the short statement of our previously stated *thesis*. To reiterate, perhaps the reason why the rural results are distinctive from the urban-based studies utilizing social disorganization and allied theories and concepts, and the reason why it appears to be less successful when tested on rural communities is that there is *no such thing as social disorganization, only forms, expressions and variations of social organization which establish the place-based contexts and conditions by which both law-abiding and criminal behaviors are expressed.*

We contend, from a critical point of view, that collective efficacy varies in strength within all places, and that it is not the opposite of social disorganization (or anti-collective efficacy) because it cannot be the opposite of something which does not exist. We posit that what all of these studies have tapped into is some aspect of social structure or social organization that either constrains or enables criminal behavior, and simultaneously does both to a considerable degree. Hence, although it is possible that at a few places some varieties of social organization are almost always associated with low crime across all of its types, and that at a few other places particular kinds of social organization go hand-in-hand with high levels of crime across all of its types, it is more likely that the diversity of social organization (multiple rural realities, and multiple urban realities as well) found in places throughout all societies of the world are simultaneously related to or associated with varying rates for specific types of crime. Hence, forms of social organization – measured as collective efficacy, cohesion, and all of the other synonyms of the same conceptual type – may reduce crime of one kind even as crime of a different variety is increased – at these same places, within the same locality-based social networks which exist within these places, and by the same individuals who reside there. Hence, why would we expect anything other than inconsistent results, limited generalizability, and a great deal of unexplained variance from this literature?[5]

A critical rural criminology working from an ecological perspective about crime would avoid the fallacies commonly found in mainstream criminological literature about social disorganization, collective efficacy, and all of the other like-minded conceptualizations. A rural critical criminological approach, as shown in Figure 3.1, would not assume a holism to the social and cultural context of a place. It would recognize that actors may occupy a diversity of statuses – as victim, offender, and law-abiding citizen – at the same time and in the same place. We are referring here to ordinary people and local elites who both uphold a social order of conformity and control for some crimes, while they themselves tolerate, consider insignificant, or engage in other forms of offending or injustice, as well as members of a community who are more full-time or chronic offenders (Chavez, Edward, & Oetting, 1989; Huff, 1996; Oetting, Edwards, Kelly, & Beauvais, 1997). There is not a simple dichotomy between a homogeneous aggregation of law-abiding citizens and a homogenous aggregation of law violators. That is what the rural literature on violence against women already tells us (DeKeseredy & Schwartz, 2009; Websdale, 1998).

Second, a critical approach would not conflate control and cohesion. While control means to limit the actions of individuals through sanctions, cohesion refers to agreement of cultural meanings and reciprocity in relationships. Hence, some forms of cohesion may control local residents such that they do not report crime, as Barclay (2003) discovered in her work on agricultural crime in New South Wales, which in turn allows it to happen even more. Hegemonic patriarchy perpetuates a localized context in which violence against women can occur repeatedly, even though it may constrain other crimes, such as burglary or street robbery (DeKeseredy, Donnermeyer, & Schwartz, 2009).

Finally, by working from images of rural communities as places which are "temporally and locationally specific terrains of power and discourse" (Liepins, 2000, p. 30), we recognize the simultaneity of social organization to both constrain and enable varieties of crime in the same localities and among the same actors. An ecological perspective will almost always be part of rural criminology, but to endow the subfield with a more critical ecological view, it must recognize the diversity of cultures and networks within the same places – in other words, functional for whom/dysfunctional for whom?

In Figure 3.1 we use the square of crime to provide a conceptual sketch of a more critical approach to rural crime from a place-based perspective. We account for selective enforcement of laws by local agencies of social control and of a community's culture, plus the multi-dimensional nature of collective efficacy.

Drugs and rural realities

Like so much of the literature about rural criminology, scholarly work on drug use and drug production/trafficking in the rural context is

Police and agencies of the state	Selective responses of local police and other criminal justice and social service agencies to offenders and victims	Collective efficacy/forms of social organization related to localized expressions of criminal behavior and the social capital which may integrate networks of local offenders	Offender
Social control			Criminal act
	Localized expressions of norms, values, and beliefs associated with conforming and illegal behaviors, and community reactions to victims	Collective efficacy/forms of social organization related to the uneven vulnerability of rural peoples and communities to crime	
The public			Victim

FIGURE 3.1 The square of crime: communities and rural crime.

scattered. In fact, a large part of the research on substance use among rural populations can be found in specializations known as social psychology, the family, and youth and adolescent studies (Donnermeyer, 1992). This micro-level view of rural substance use is quite voluminous, with hundreds of studies on rural populations or comparisons of rural and urban rates of substance use and abuse (Oetting et al., 1997; Pratt, 2009; Van Gundy, 2006). It is mostly quantitative and relies on theories and models which focus on a nexus of individual and social characteristics, such as risk-seeking, adjustment in school, integration into the family, and peer associations. There is much less scholarship on larger, macro-level factors associated with substance use in rural places, and on drug production/trafficking in the rural context; however, this work is more centrally located in the criminology and criminal justice literature (Garriott, 2011; Haight et al., 2005; O'Dea, Murphy, & Balzer, 1997;Weisheit, 1992, 2008; Weisheit & Fuller, 2004), and more qualitative in orientation. Notwithstanding these divergent strands of literature, when woven together, they point toward a picture of rural areas which address critically all four mythologies about rural crime.

Rural peoples around the world have never been immune from using substances which are harmful, illegal, or both (Edwards & Donnermeyer, 2002). The harm is not only personal, but familial, communal, and even society wide (Donnermeyer, 1997; Kelleher & Robbins, 1997). Rural–urban comparisons of rates of illicit substances are hard to come by for most countries, but a study in the U.S. from the University of Michigan, called the "Monitoring the Future" (MTF) study, offers a vivid picture of comparative substance use. This study has taken a snapshot of the alcohol and other drug use by American youth every year since 1976, hence, longitudinal comparisons are possible as well. What the data from MTF demonstrate is that there are very few differences in rates of use between rural and urban youth today, and for some substances, the rates are higher for adolescents from rural localities.

Even though the study itself has one substantial weakness – it is a self-report survey of students who have remained in school and have not dropped-out – the multi-year picture is revealing. Thirty years ago, during the early years of MTF, rates were always higher for urban youth, and frequently, much higher. Today, for most substances, including alcohol, marijuana, cocaine, inhalants, and methamphetamines, rural youth show higher rates of use, and it has been this way for most of the past ten years (Johnston, O'Malley, Bachman, & Schulenberg, 2012).

Rural adult populations also show substantial usage (Robertson & Donnermeyer, 1997, 1998), even though more recent reports from the large National Survey on Drug Use and Health (NSDUH) show rates of use to be somewhat lower again among residents in non-metropolitan counties (Substance Abuse and Mental Health Services Administration, 2012). This report found a higher risk of alcohol abuse than substance abuse for most rural adults, especially among Native Americans, which has also been documented by other researchers (Wood, 2009), and higher rates of substance use for young rural males than females, for rural people who are unmarried and have less education, and for both Hispanic American and African American populations as well.

The Carsey Institute's report (Van Gundy, 2006) on rural substance abuse concludes "that rural and urban places today have similar rates of substance use and abuse, and, for abuse of some substances, rural Americans are at an even higher risk than their urban counterparts" (p. 4). The MTF, the NSDUH, and the Carsey Institute report may be specific to the United States, but their conclusions can be applied worldwide, at least to some degree. In an edited special issue of the journal *Substance Use and Misuse* (Edwards & Donnermeyer, 2002), studies of alcohol and drug abuse by youth and adults from the rural regions of societies around the world were published, including Yoruba women in Nigeria (Mamman, Brieger, & Oshiname, 2002), Arab and Jewish rural youth in northern Israel (Weiss, 2002), the relationship of social cohesion and adolescent drug use in various rural communities of Mexico (Wagner, Dia, López, Collado, & Aldaz, 2002), and a combined historical and contemporary overview among people who live in the western highlands of Scotland (Dean, 2002). As well, Bull's (2007) and Hogg and Carrington's (2006) research on rural Australia show alcohol and substance abuse to be more problematic in many rural localities than in the urban context.

Stallwitz (2012) and Stallwitz and Shewan (2004) examined the Shetland Islands of northern Scotland, describing the changing social and cultural contexts of heroin use there. The insights from their work have relevance for understanding the social organization (i.e., collective efficacy) of substance use across all rural places:

> The scene surrounding the purchase and consumption of heroin has traditionally been extremely secretive and controlled, involving a small underground group whose heroin use has been carefully hidden from day-to-day public life. However, recent developments suggest not only a greater and easier availability and increasing prevalence of heroin on the island and a growing number of more diverse users, but also the beginning of a diminishing of the severity of the stigma attached to heroin use.... It is important to place these developments in the context of the use of other drugs on the island. The excessive consumption of alcohol seems to constitute a socially desirable and shared cultural experience for the Shetland population as a whole, virtually regardless of gender, generation or social status.
>
> *(Stallwitz & Shewan, 2004, p. 375)*

A similar depiction of social organization, representing a web of users, dealers, and producers can be found in Barton, Story and Palmer's (2011) description of the rural areas in the county of Cornwall, located in the south-western tip of England. Due to its coastline, Cornwall is the frequent location for drug drop-offs smuggled into the United Kingdom from other countries, and has several centuries of smuggling experience, forming a large share of its economic history (Waugh, 1991). The illicit drugs are transported to a number of large cities throughout the country. However, as they observe:

> Once in the county, these large shipments are then transported to major cities such as Bristol, Liverpool and Manchester for national distribution. Ironically, they are often transported back to the county to be sold.... It is also the case that dealing networks are often spread between adjacent towns.
>
> *(Barton et al., 2011, p. 153)*

Their description shows the extent to which a diversity of localized social structures, all with strong expressions of collective efficacy, exist in the same places with individuals who are law-abiding, a point which is also apparent in the work of Stallwitz (2012) and Stallwitz and Shewan (2004).

This kind of analysis is important if one is to adopt a critical look at rural substance use. The reason is that the fundamental etiology of substance use is the same for both rural and urban populations, regardless of gender, age, race/ethnicity, and various social factors associated with family, peers, schools, and work (Conger, 1997; Donnermeyer & Scheer, 2001; Oetting et al., 1997; Scheer, Borden, & Donnermeyer, 2000; Gfroerer, Larson, & Colliver, 2007; Van Gundy, 2006; Wilson & Donnermeyer, 2006). A litany of individual and interpersonal factors can be listed to explain individual choices to use and misuse substances, and to engage in various illegal behaviors related to illicit substances. There may well be minor rural–urban differences in the size of a beta coefficient for one of the variables which predicts substance use, after controlling for a host of other factors in any form of multivariate analysis (Oetting et al., 1997; Scheer et al., 2000; Wilson & Donnermeyer, 2006), but the reality is that rural–urban differences in etiology are of little consequence until structural realities are addressed. In other words, the advice of Jock Young (2011) quoted at the beginning of this chapter is sound. The sum total of all of these studies confirms there are minimal rural–urban differences in substance use etiology, but fails to bring a larger, structural and more critical understanding to the scholarly examination of substance use and drug production/trafficking in the rural context.

Consider, for example, the case of Harlan County, Kentucky, in Box 3.1 below, which is taken from the Carsey Institute Report (Van Gundy, 2006), or of the conclusions from studies in the Shetland Islands (Stallwitz, 2012; Stallwitz & Shewan, 2004). Both point to a rural reality (Donnermeyer & Tunnell, 2007) which belies the assumptions underlying social disorganization theory, even when it is invoked to explain substance use in the rural context (Baker, 2008; Hayes-Smith & Whaley, 2009; Oetting, Donnermeyer, & Deffenbacher, 1998). What the research on rural substance use describes over and over again, when it considers community and societal-level factors rather than individual and interpersonal level variables, is the ways that social organization of the rural is changing, either from within or from the outside. For example, in rural areas where unemployment and seasonal employment are more enduring, especially among young males (Sherman, 2005), and in the relative geographic and cultural insularity of some rural communities, one response is the development of oppositional behaviors as expressions of masculinity (Stough-Hunter, 2010). In turn, this can translate into men (and women) engaging in more risky behaviors, a cultural context not dissimilar to the patriarchy which helps us understand intimate partner violence in the rural context (DeKeseredy & Schwartz, 2009; Carrington et al., 2011).

A variety of community level factors, familiar because of their frequent mention as antecedent variables in social disorganization theory (Havens et al., 2011; Hayes-Smith & Whaley, 2009; Oetting et al., 1998), help set the stage for understanding rural community context and substance use. From national level studies, such as the NSDUH and MTF, to more localized rural-based studies (Draus & Carlson, 2006; Leukefeld, Logan, Farabee, & Clayton, 2002), research indicates the extreme importance of networks in the social learning and sustained use of harmful and illegal substances among rural (and urban) populations (Oetting & Donnermeyer, 1998). Users often travel back and forth between their rural (or former) rural hometowns and larger communities, where they work and/or party, sharing needles and engaging in other risky and even criminal behaviors. Often, they carry health risks, as well as modeling attitudes and behaviors about substances, back to their rural origins and to family members and friends who still live there. Further, the behaviors are more risky because health and counseling services are often lacking in the rural areas (Leukefeld et al., 2002; Webster, Malteyoke-Scrivner, Staton, & Leukefeld, 2007).

Economic disadvantage (poverty, unemployment, underemployment), population change (increases as outsiders move in or decreases due to economic downturns), family instability, improved transportation systems (or its opposite, geographic isolation), lack of law enforcement, and a host of other community level factors have been cited as contributing to the development of drug networks (Baker, 2008). However, in order to truly appreciate how collective efficacy can enable crime as much as constrain it, and how threads of social organization are interwoven at the same places, the criminological literature on drug production in the rural context must be consulted. Further, when the individual level and social-psychological level studies are considered in tandem with the more criminologically oriented rural literature on drug production and trafficking, then the myths about rural crime are really not so benign.

Illegal production of substances has been part of the rural scene for a very long time (Weisheit et al., 2006). Making moonshine or distilled whiskey is most popularly associated with rural Appalachia in the U.S.A. In states like Kentucky and Tennessee, where thousands of jobs are associated with bourbon/whiskey production, a majority of the non-metropolitan counties remain "dry" to this day, which means the sale of alcohol is prohibited. It could be claimed that this historical arrangement, whereby a few companies, like Jack Daniels, can legally produce alcohol for sale across the globe, but local people are prohibited from buying it, pushing both production and its consumption into the backwoods and up the hollows (i.e., narrow valleys), has other functions as well. Not only is this reality supportive of illegal, moonshine production, but it helps to maintain a folklore-like status of moonshiners as a form of rebellion by rural people living deep in the Appalachian hills against the intrusion of big government in the form of the "revenoor." Revenoor is a slang term for a U.S. government revenue agent, who, along with state and local law enforcement, sought to shut down these operations, which were technically illegal. Today, moonshine is assimilated into the economy through tourist sales of alcohol under its nickname of "white-lightening," a popular television series with highly misrepresentative depictions of rural culture and rural people, *Dukes of Hazzard*, and more recently, the Discovery Channel's so-called reality show, *Moonshiners*, which is set in western Virginia around a country town with the unlikely name of Climax.

Another nearly indigenous form of drug production in many rural regions of the world, including the United States, is marijuana cultivation (Weisheit, 1992). Distinctive from moonshine production, which can be understood in part as a clash of cultural values and governmentality (Garland, 1996), marijuana production takes on stronger features of organized crime and rural–urban linkages relative to distribution and trafficking. Marijuana requires a growing medium, which can range from a small plot of land hidden deep in the back country or surrounded by a field of corn or other taller plants, to a sophisticated and expensive greenhouse operation.

Moonshine and marijuana are like country cousins from the point of view that many of the producers and traffickers are local, rural people who express strong oppositional views to the intrusiveness of "big government," a cultural theme that runs through the context of understanding a wider variety of rural-based crime and deviance issues, such as racist/hate groups and violence against women (Weisheit et al., 2006). However, marijuana takes on a greater significance because it more substantially undergirds the economy of some rural counties whose above-ground economies are weak and rates of poverty are high, and because it creates new forms of social organization through distribution pipelines to urban populations and links to other forms of crime, such as prostitution and cocaine (Lyman & Potter, 1998; Potter & Gaines, 1992; Weisheit et al., 2006). Also, marijuana production can be very lucrative, including the famous case of the "cornbread mafia" bust in eastern Kentucky, which was in fact a group of producers with sites in numerous states, making millions of dollars (Coates & Weingarten, 1990). Similarly, Lyman and Potter's (1998) overview of marijuana production and trafficking, while not explicitly focused on the rural, continuously refers to rural places as integrated into a global underground network. In fact, they refer to the business side of marijuana production as a "somewhat fragmented group of traffickers who rely on kinship or local ('good ole boy') networks" (Lyman & Potter, 1998, p. 154). Lyman and Potter's description shows the extent to which a diversity of localized social structures, all with strong expressions of collective efficacy, exist in the same places alongside other networks of people who do not or rarely break the law, and including, of course, individuals who participate in both (Stallwitz, 2012; Stallwitz & Shewan, 2004) Later, when we review from a critical point of view the research on agricultural crime, behaviors of individuals like these will be referred to as "pluriactivity."

There is little systematic research on the development of gangs in rural places, despite the legendary status of criminal gangs in the frontier lore of the U.S. West in the 1800s, and the re-emergence of gangster popularity during the Bonnie and Clyde and John Derringer days of the 1920s and 1930s, much of which took place in small towns and the open-country areas of the midwestern region of the U.S.A. In counterdistinction, the work of Clinard (1942, 1944) and others (Clark & Wenninger, 1962; Esselstyn, 1953; Ferdinand, 1964; Gibbons, 1972; Wiers, 1939), representing some of the earliest empirical research in rural criminology, mostly claimed that rural offenders were more isolated, both geographically and socially, engaging in various forms of criminal activity alone. An exception to the early work on rural offenders was Hardman (1996), who interviewed gang members in a small town in the state of Wisconsin and concluded there were few differences between them and those who belonged to gangs in big cities. The view of the rural offender as a social isolate helps perpetuate the myth that rural areas have less crime because they exhibit more cohesion or collective efficacy. Those who do violate the law are not typical, and as exceptions or aberrations, any explanation of their behavior must be based on individual-level traits, and not expressions of a rural locality's social organization and culture. Perhaps also the early work was more true at the time the research was completed and for the locations where the studies were conducted; nonetheless, what the early criminological research failed to do was to link their findings to anything about the rural context, either historically or contemporaneously. Hence, they failed to use their criminological imaginations.

Times change, however, and rural criminological work today points to a picture whereby some rural areas exhibit forms of social networks linked to very organized forms of criminal activity in association with substance use and misuse. It may not be in the form of media stereotypes of the urban, such as "home-boys" and drive-by shootings, but it certainly exists. One area where the diffusion thesis – the idea, as Fischer (1980) proposed, that crime diffuses from urban to rural places, hence, rural places "lag behind" urban places in expressions of crime – is the more recent development of gangs associated with drug production and trafficking in rural communities (Donnermeyer, 1994; Dukes & Stein, 2003; Weisheit et al., 2006).

The evidence is scanty because the amount of research is limited, but what it does suggest is that new forms of social organization and collective efficacy have developed, centered around drug production and trafficking in the rural context, with associated rural–urban links in distribution networks. For example, Wells and Weisheit (2001) discovered that gang members sometimes move to smaller places because they move with their families, in part because families are seeking to remove themselves from more dangerous urban places, or because of factory relocation and other forms of rural economic change. Donnermeyer

(1994) interviewed rural law enforcement officers and discovered hints for four models of gang development in the rural context, even though his research was insufficient to be conclusive. These include: (1) displacement, whereby gang members, with or without their families, relocate to small towns (often moving in with extended family) within easy travelling distance of a big city to escape possible harm by competing gangs or enforcement efforts by city police; (2) the branch office, whereby city-based gangs establish a presence in a small town as a transportation hub for regional/national/international distribution; (3) the franchise, whereby local dealers link up with larger and established city-based gangs in order to gain greater access to a wider variety of drugs for redistribution back in the their small towns; and (4) social learning, whereby local rural offenders, especially juveniles, while in detention centers, establish links with juveniles who belong to city-located gangs, who are also serving time; hence, with their improved "cultural capital" (i.e., knowledge about distribution/gang organization/types of drugs) and "social capital" (greater access to networks), these rural youth improve the organization of drug-dealing back in their rural hometowns and gain leadership and authority within these criminal cliques.

Regardless of the model, the evidence suggests that new forms of social organization and new and/or modified forms of social control occur as illicit substances diffuse into a community, rural or urban, for the first time (Evans, Fitzgerald, Weigel, & Chvilicek, 1999; Weisheit et al., 2006). Consider, for example, the spread of OxyContin and methamphetamines into the rural scene. Box 3.1, which is abridged from the Carsey Institute Report (Van Gundy, 2006), shows how drug abuse spreads into a rural locality, and paints a dramatic picture of profits and pills. What began as a form of worker exploitation by coal companies metamorphosed into a significant part of the county's economic, social and cultural life. Harlan County continues as a high poverty county with few prospects for the development of businesses and industries not dependent on coal. Even so, its social organization has diversified, forming new patterns in association with the entry of OxyContin and other drugs into the area. Today, the slang term for OxyContin, illustrating its concentration in rural areas, is "hillbilly heroin."

Box 3.1 Excerpts from "Hard Times in Harlan" by Bill Bishop

In the fall of 2005, Harlan, Kentucky, put on a play about its struggles with drug addiction – a battle that the community has so far lost.

A key scene in Harlan's community drama, *Higher Ground*, became known as the "drug zombie dance." The chorus, playing the zombies, stumbles and staggers onto the stage chanting:

I've got a pain, I've got a pain.
I've got a pain in my hip,
In my back, in my neck…
In my soul.
And I'm searching for a cure to take my pain away.

Harlan County lies at the extreme southeast corner of Kentucky. Harlan is the most famous coal county in the nation. In the 1930s, Harlan ("Bloody Harlan" back then) was the center of union organizing efforts by both the Communist Party USA and the United Mine Workers of America…. In the 1970s, the county was the backdrop for the mine strike viewed by the nation in the Academy Award-winning documentary, *Harlan County, USA.*

People here still talk coal, about the big strip mines that sheared off the tops of mountains the underground operations created to satisfy the country's demand for cheaper energy. But more often they talk about drugs; in particular they tell stories about the painkiller OxyContin.

The "drug zombie" scene in *Higher Ground* hints at the source of Harlan's uniquely pervasive drug problem:

"In the past, coal miners spent hours each day crouched in narrow mine shafts," concluded a 2002 report by the U.S. Department of Justice. "Painkillers were dispensed by mining camp doctors in an attempt to keep the miners working. Self-medicating became a way of life for miners."

(Lexington Herald-Leader December 7, 2003)

The drug graduated from prescribed painkiller to addictive drug when users discovered how to remove the time-release coating and use the drug to obtain a powerful and addictive high. Once OxycContin made the leap from disabled miners to the rest of the population, users began experimenting, mixing the painkiller with other drugs. The county was overwhelmed. A candidate for Harlan County sheriff, who was apparently negotiating a deal for protection, was shot and his body was burned by drug dealers.

... a "listening project" (funded by the Rockefeller Foundation...) conducted over 450 interviews with residents. The stories are mixture of hopelessness and horror... A young single mother says:

The Xanax, at first I used it to help me cope, and later found if you took two you would feel good and later realized if I drank on it I felt really good.

A middle-aged woman with four years of college says:

Doctors and drug companies feed us drugs just like giving a baby candy.... It's so bad that I can no longer trust some people in my own family. They steal from you – lie. You never know who is on drugs ... people drooling ... taking from their parents and children. It's awful.

Abridged from insert reading – "Hard Times in Harlan" – pp. 20–21 in Van Gundy, 2006.

Methamphetamine production is another such example. Even during the 1960s and 1970s, when marijuana and other hallucinatory drugs were becoming a more visible feature of many societies around the world, few would have predicted the consequences of methamphetamines in rural areas (Donnermeyer & Tunnell, 2007). Methamphetamines were used during World War II to help long-range bomber pilots stay awake, and to treat various physical ailments, such as asthma, obesity, and sinus problems. Early versions were used as speed and pep pills, and as a stimulant, which fits well with 20th- and 21st-century lifestyles (Mehling, 2008). Methamphetamines can be ingested in a variety of ways, and can be produced easily by trained chemists and self-trained amateurs (Weisheit, 2008). The chemicals used for its production can pose extreme hazards to the maker's health, to those living in the same building, and to the surrounding environment, especially groundwater (Weisheit, 2008). Thousands of websites are available which describe the various ways it can be made.

Large-scale production of methamphetamine in the United States first developed on the west coast, especially San Francisco, spreading to the south and southwest, and then to the midwest. The drug is commonly associated with the movement of Mexican immigrants, both legal and illegal, as farm laborers, landscape workers, and workers in meat-packing plants. However, it is also true that many hundreds of rural communities include local "mom and pop" producers, working out of their homes and in wooded or isolated areas nearby (O'Dea et al., 1997; Weisheit, 2008), mimicking the subterfuge practiced by both moonshiners and marijuana growers. The number of methamphetamine lab seizures is generally higher in rural areas than urban areas, with various rural states, such as Missouri, claiming a dubious supremacy for the largest number (O'Dea et al., 1997; Donnermeyer & Tunnell, 2007).

Regardless of how OxyContin, methamphetamine, and other highly addictive substances are used and abused by rural populations, and no matter how slowly or quickly systems for its production and consumption develop within rural communities, inevitably these new forms of social organization and collective efficacy become part of the local ecology. A study (Carbone-Lopez, Gatewood Owens, & Miller, 2012) from rural Missouri of incarcerated women found a pattern familiar to scholars who examine other forms of drug use in the rural context. Most of these women learned about and initiated use in private settings, such as someone's home. In addition, these women came from families where other members use and misuse substances, and in numerous cases, learning and using highlight an intergenerational transmission of attitudes and behaviors. As Haight et al. (2005) discovered in their study of methamphetamine's impact on family and children in rural Illinois: "children may be taught directly to lie to teachers, police officers and child welfare workers to cover their parent's illegal activities" (p. 959).

Garriott's (2011) case study of a rural area in the state of West Virginia shows how methamphetamine production and use become as pervasive as the competition for blue-ribbons for the best apple pie at a county fair. The local pharmacist is among the first in the community to become aware of locals who are using. Locals who are addicted often become dealers, sell off their property, and steal from extended family members to support their habits. Conservation officers in nearby state and national parks and forestland are confronted with lab discoveries, the dangers associated with investigating these clandestine operations, environmental degradation, and the financial costs of clean-up. A house burned down in the community that was a methamphetamine lab. It is a regular topic of conversation in the basement of churches when locals meet for coffee and refreshments after a Sunday service or a bible studies class. And the local police deal with the effects of methamphetamine addiction and production continuously, either directly or indirectly, through everything they do as officers in a small community where people are likely to know each other and to know them personally. One deputy described how he frequently would confront people about their addiction who had suddenly lost weight, or had a large scab on their face, or looked high as they walked on the street or while driving a motor vehicle. Garriott (2011) evokes an image of rural which hardly fits the idyll as he summarizes the impact of methamphetamines on a state trooper who is part of a Federal Drug Task Force in his area:

> In addition to witnessing the extremes to which people would go in order to satisfy their addition, he had had to come to terms with the extensiveness of the problems in his community – the sheer numbers of people who used the drug or were involved in making and selling it. He found all of this very challenging, particularly as he tried to lead a normal life outside of work. "It's hard," he said, "especially when you're out with your family. I can take you to any street anywhere in the area, including the dirt roads, and show you someone who's using or selling drugs. It makes you wonder, 'Where have all the good people gone?'"

(p. 57)

Even though the literature on substance use, production, and trafficking with a rural focus is largely from the United States, the implications are global. Production and distribution of illicit substances is a globalized commodity chain of inputs and finished products, with complex systems of distribution (Lyman & Potter, 1998). As Thoumi (2005) observed about drug production from a worldwide perspective: "The illegal industry developed in this area mainly because institutions were weak, state legitimacy was challenged by many excluded from power, and law enforcement was ineffective and arbitrary." (p. 196).

One of the most important contributions that critical criminology can make to mainstream criminology is to reframe criminological research in ways that illustrate the structural conditions of crime, especially forms of inequality, racism, and sexism, and to show how the micro and the macro are related. In the previous chapter we contended that the square of crime was not outmoded, but was a valuable rubric for understanding rural crime (Donnermeyer & DeKeseredy, 2008). Putting aside for the moment arguments about legalization of various controlled substances, moral panic about drugs, and the cost of government efforts to "wage war" on drugs, drug use, and trafficking/production in rural places, the square of crime shows how a critical perspective is advantageous (see Figure 3.2). The cause of drug use behavior, that is, the etiology of use, shows little difference between rural and urban environments. However, these personal and interpersonal factors interact or vector with factors related to the vulnerability of local populations/communities (unemployment, systemic drug use associated with an occupation, local forms of illegal drug production, and networks of distribution, etc.) to create high levels of use at some rural places. Awareness and tolerance of substance use and localized forms of production and distribution (Donnermeyer et al., 1997) changes people's perceptions of their hometowns and how individuals at the local level interact with each other (Van Gundy, 2006; Garriott, 2011). In turn, both local law enforcement and state/national governmental entities play a role through the establishment of laws which make some substances illegal, and through selective enforcement. As well, the presence of organized crime affects local law enforcement and the effects of addictive behaviors ripples through the entire social and cultural fabric of rural communities.

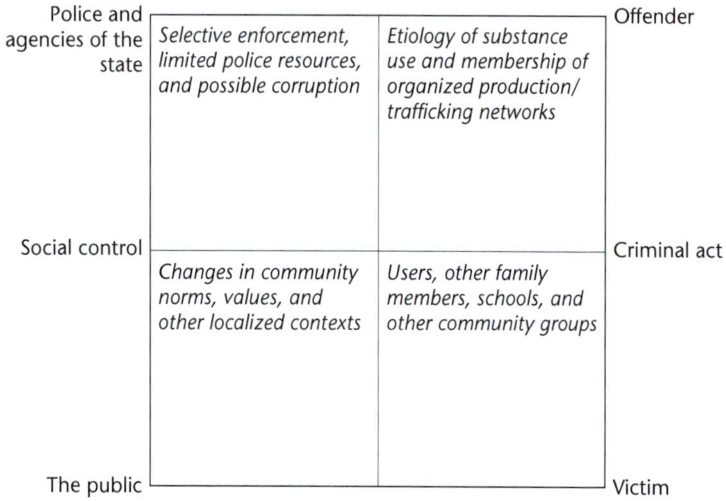

FIGURE 3.2 The square of crime: drugs and rural realities.

The four rural myths from Chapter 1 can be challenged from a variety of perspectives, and the rural criminology of substance use, misuse, production, and trafficking is one way to accomplish their *coup de grace*. For one, not all rural communities are alike, and they are changing as continuously and fundamentally as urban places, something a rural–urban dichotomy fails to recognize. The rise of serious drug abuse, such as marijuana, OxyContin, and methamphetamines, shows how the flow of population and labor underpins economies, both above-ground and underground. Rural communities are not simply filled with "the good ole boys, never meaning no harm."[6] For boys and girls, women and men, substance use has real consequences, and drug production and trafficking is localized organized crime with global linkages.

Second, the rise of substance use and illegal drug production in the rural is not a story of disorder and disorganization, but of sustained social networks which are new forms of social organization and collective efficacy, which, in turn, enable addictive behaviors and a new kind of economic base at the local level. Hence, the rural research, from the Shetland Islands (Stallwitz, 2012; Stallwitz & Shewan, 2004) to Harlan County (Van Gundy, 2006), indicates that another false dichotomy is the idea that disorganization or some haphazard reference to "anti-collective effi-cacy" has any scientific value for interpreting the data (quantitative or qualitative) from a theoretical/conceptual point of view. A weakened economy and the diminishing of other previously strong forms of social control at rural places does not indicate disorder, but rather a shift or change to new social orders (Sherman, 2012; Thuomi, 2005).

Third, the research on substance use, drug production/trafficking, and gang emergence does indeed suggest the idea that a diffusion approach can have value. The focus of Garriott's (2011) work was "narcopolitics" as expressed at the local level, recognizing the role of global networks of production and trafficking, and the role of laws, governments, and the police in how offenders behave and how violations of the law are enforced. The sum of Garriott's (2011) work and of all the research, however, does not assume anything about rural rates being historically low, but illustrates simply that crime does not happen instantaneously across all places. It has an ecology, and understanding ecological patterns from a critical perspective contributes to a broader understanding of the structural forces underlying crime in both the rural and urban sectors of societies around the world. Consider, for example, the rates of substance use among 12th grade students from the Monitoring the Future Study, as it has tracked changes from 1976 to the present (Johnston et al., 2012). Sometimes urban rates are higher, and sometimes rural rates are higher for both overall use and for specific kinds of illicit substances. It is impossible to say who lags behind who, for what type of drug, and where the early users lived when compared to later users.

Finally, the image of the rural as idyllic persists in the criminological literature. Yet, there is a long history of rural places as the prime locali-ties for organized forms of illegal behavior, from moonshine to meth-amphetamine. Putting aside the debate about the government's role in arbitrarily or unfairly defining alcohol, marijuana, and other drugs as illegal, the research shows beyond that proverbial "shadow of a doubt" that rural places are inhabited by people who display a complicated mix of conforming and criminal behaviors. To repeat a recurring claim made throughout this chapter and this book, threaded seamlessly through the tapestry of any rural place are forms of social organization which allow its members to simultaneously participate in both conforming/legal activities and deviant behaviors which are illegal.

Agricultural crime[7]

In many countries, agriculture is a high-tech, capital-intensive, multi-billion dollar industry, yet one that has defied a common feature of capitalism, as the vast majority of operations, even the largest, are still family (not stockholder) owned (Lobao & Meyer, 2001). Despite this feature, however, agriculture today is as "business" in its orientation as any other sector in the economies of advanced capitalist countries. It should not be surprising that losses from agricultural crime in the U.S.A. alone are estimated at several billion dollars annually (Donnermeyer, 2012).

Agriculturalists are not only targets of crime, but they also commit many "crimes of the powerful" (Pearce, 1976). First, though, let's consider agricultural crime from the victim's point of view. There is a number of victimization studies conducted in Australia, England, Scotland, and the U.S.A. over the past 30 years. Using mid-range figures from a recent review of agricultural crime studies (Donnermeyer et al., 2011), it is estimated that each year, machinery and equipment theft occurs to about 18% of farm operations, and a similar proportion are affected by incidents of vandalism that are costly, in terms of both replacement of property and disruption of daily operations to repair damaged property. About 8% of food producers suffer the theft of some type of livestock, and perhaps most telling of all, approximately 9% experience the breaking and entering of a farm building, a rate that far exceeds most rates of burglary for urban neighborhoods in countries like Canada and the United States (Barclay & Donnermeyer, 2011). Incidences of trespassing can also be high and damage caused by hunters or those who use large ranch and farmlands for illegal marijuana, methamphetamine, and other forms of drug production is also prevalent in some rural regions (Barclay & Donnermeyer, 2011; Donnermeyer & Tunnell, 2007; Garriott, 2011; Weisheit & Fuller, 2004).

These rates of victimization should not be surprising when viewed from a critical perspective (DeKeseredy & Donnermeyer, 2013), and the changing ecology of farm crime is vital to making this link. For example, the location of a break and enter into a farm building varies by its visibility to the agricultural operator plus the value of machinery, equipment, and supplies stored in the facility. A building closer to the farm homestead is less likely to be burglarized because it is easier for the farmer and the farmer's family to notice suspicious activity. A building farther away, and out of sight of the homestead, is much easier prey for the person intent on breaking in. As well, the value of the stored items and the ability of the thief to convert what is stolen to cash affect the likelihood of farm burglary (Donnermeyer et al., 2010; Hedayati, 2008). Agricultural operations located near public roads are more accessible and more likely to experience various forms of theft, illegal dumping, vandalism, and trespassing (Barclay & Donnermeyer, 2011). Plus, many agricultural areas are subject to forms of urbanization brought about by the consumption of rural landscapes by tourists and recreationalists (Krannich & Petrzelka, 2003; Lichter & Brown, 2011), suburban and industrial developments, and a host of other economic and cultural factors that increasingly tie together the rural and urban sectors of many societies (Brown & Schafft, 2011). Farms and ranches are no longer, and have really never been, as isolated – physically, culturally, and socially – as portrayed by agrarian fundamentalism.

The intersection of offenders and victims is thus as applicable to understanding agricultural crime as it would be to crime in the city. In the strands of mainstream criminology known as CPTED (crime prevention through environmental design) and situational crime prevention, factors impacting visibility or surveillance are known as a form of "guardianship" (Donnermeyer, 2007a; Felson & Bora, 2010). However, the ecological patterns discovered through studies of farm victimization point to an essential feature of agricultural crime that could best interpreted from a critical approach, such as a left realist perspective, which links the micro and the macro. Traditional interpretations of Marxist theory argued that farming would follow an industrial model, with the eventual proletarianization of farm labor under the control of a small class of owners (Mann & Dickinson, 1978). However, a complete transformation did not occur (Lobao & Meyer, 2001; Mooney, 1988). Instead, family forms of agricultural production persist in advanced capitalist societies, creating a large number of independent producers, even as the majority of food producers from former times sold out or were pushed out by these same economic forces, leaving for non-farm jobs often located in nearby urban centers.

The family basis of contemporary agriculture is one reason why the ideology of agrarian fundamentalism persists today. The reality, however, is that much of farming in advanced capitalist societies today has adopted a Fordist or industrialized mode of production in order to survive (Lobao & Meyer, 2001; Pfeffer, 1984). Hence, a left realist approach views farmers and ranchers not merely as simple producers of food commodities who are occasionally victimized by a thief, burglar, or trespasser. They are industrialists who produce food through capital-intensive production methods, embedded within a globalized market system. These structural transformations to agriculture create a greater likelihood of farm victimization which is both frequent and expensive. Consider, for example, one nine-county area of California, where millions of dollars in theft illustrate not only the high cost of agricultural crime, but its industrialized features (Donnermeyer et al., 2011). Items stolen included barbed wire fencing, saddles and other tack associated with both recreational and work horses, irrigation pipes, water pumps, welders, diesel and other kinds of fuel, various livestock, fertilizer, pesticides and herbicides, and ripened fruit from groves of trees and bushes.

In reassessing the potential of left realism as a form of critical criminology, DeKeseredy and Schwartz (2006) observed, "Of course, we don't know what left realists would say about terrorist attacks" (p. 312). Jennifer Gibbs (2010) now has something to say. She asserts that left realist theory is useful in explaining why it is that economically disenfranchised men and women engage in terrorist acts. Especially in rural areas, militant right-wing, anti-government groups are more likely to emerge in areas where there are high levels of unemployment. Also, for Gibbs, the influence of terrorist leaning subcultures helps us understand why terrorism is no better fought with "get tough" policies than is street crime. The deterrent effect of arrest and punishment is weak and ineffective against those who justify their actions based on deep-set beliefs and values reinforced by others who feel the same. From a left realist perspective, Gibbs' insights mark the start of work on agro-terrorism, which is a major threat to many farms around the world. Increasingly, farms are targets for politically motivated attempts to instill fear and to sabotage food production by both domestic and international groups (Donnermeyer et al., 2011; Moats, 2007). Many agriculturalists and the industrialized forms of farming they operate are symbols of a ruling class and of the hegemonic nature of capitalist production that puts many rural localities at an economic and political disadvantage.

A left realist approach sees agriculturalists themselves as situated in complex webs of economic, political, and social class relations that blur the distinction between victim and offender. For example, a combined quantitative-qualitative study in Australia discovered a pattern which indicated a surprising degree of neighbor-to-neighbor victimization that was enabled precisely by the type of *Gemeinschaft* relations that many mainstream criminologists presume to be expressions of collective effi- cacy and that supposedly describe neighborhoods with relatively little crime (Barclay, 2003; Donnermeyer, 2007b; Sampson et al., 1998). Victims considered the impact of reporting a crime, especially stock theft, allegedly committed by a farmer-neighbor in small agricultural communities where norms may create forms of ostracism against those who "dob in" or snitch to the police. In turn, the police practiced considerable discretion about responding to reports of stock theft based on the relative social standings of both the victim and the suspected offender within the community (Barclay et al., 2004). These place- based dynamics are not unlike those documented by DeKeseredy and associates in their examination of intimate partner violence, even though the two crimes are completely different types (DeKeseredy et al., 2006; DeKeseredy & Schwartz, 2009).

Not only are agriculturalists subject to forms of street (or shall we say "country lane") crime, but a left realist approach would give equal attention to agricultural crime as illustrative of crimes of the powerful. The phrase "food regimes" was created by sociologists who study agri- culture to describe the place of food producers within internationalized forms of complex commodity production that extend beyond the means of the state to regulate in terms of environmental policies, labor laws, and the price/distribution of food (Buttel & Goodman, 1989; Fried- mann, 1993; McMichael, 2008). It can also be used to relocate agricul- turalists within the square of crime, but this time as offenders, not victims.

There are two potential forms of offending among agriculturalists. First, agriculturalists can be simultaneously engaged in both legitimate and illegal activities. This form of pluriactivity (McElwee, Smith, & Somerville, 2011) refers to farmers and ranchers who grow crops and raise livestock for the marketplace, but are also involved in various types of criminal activities. Some of these involve theft by farmers from other farmers, such as described in the work by Barclay (2003). Another set of activities include agriculturalists' use of their land and resources for drug production (Donnermeyer & Tunnell, 2007; Weisheit, 1992). Still other activities encompass violations of regulations related to both flora and fauna. Previously, these might have been described as a type of "folk crime" (Gibbons, 1972), that is, as localized expressions of oppositional behaviors by agriculturalists in response to state imposed gaming and other laws, reflecting their rootedness in forms of private property rights and control over the land they own (Weisheit et al., 2006). In actual fact, many food producers who are involved in these activities are integrated into complex networks engaged in various forms of transnational crimes (White, 2011). A left realist approach sees pluraiactivity as a rationalized form (Mooney, 1988) of exploitative behavior, and would seek to link the specific or micro expressions of crime committed by agriculturalists to broader, structural characteristics of societies, which is where ultimate solutions and policy recommendations must occur.

Further, most farmers are not simply autonomous producers of food who act on their own to make a living for their family, as an agrarian fundamentalist frame would describe it, but as members of a privileged capitalist class who approach profit and efficiency in much the same way as any other business firm would (Lobao & Meyer, 2001). Often, they are the local elites who react to economic, social, and political pressures that extend well beyond their home communities (Lichter & Brown, 2011; McMichael, 2008). Hence, for the agriculturalist as offender, behavior is not situated within local norms, but in worldwide markets for goods and services, and associated state-sponsored regulatory features of these systems. The work of Walters (2004, 2006) points to how a left realist approach to the study of farm crime can situate certain agricultural operations as specific places where forms of corporate crime related to the control of genetically modified organisms (GMOs) and the monopolization of seeds are carried out. Walters has stressed the geopolitical forces that threaten family-based farming systems in many countries, and the resultant growth of international corporations who are able to monopolize systems of raising crops and animals. Within these battles over the control of seed and living organisms, and concerns over the biological and environmental impacts of GMOs, are family-based food producers themselves, and how they fare. Taking the side of firms that seek monopolization of food production places some agriculturalists squarely as the local agents in corporate forms of biological crime, that is, crimes of the powerful.

Another variant of crimes of the powerful within the agricultural realm is the exploitation and victimization of farm labor. Consider Basran, Gill, and MacLean's (1995) Canadian local survey of corporate violence against Punjabi farmworkers and their children. This influenced Kwantlen Polytechnic University and the British Columbia government to provide suitable and affordable childcare for Punjabi farmworkers. As well, studies in other countries note the exploitative characteristics of owner–farmworker relations, especially with migrant labor (Rothenberg, 1998; Rye & Andrzejewska, 2010). Still, as Weisheit et al. (2006) observed, studies of rural crime have largely ignored the victimization of farmworkers.

Hence, a left realist approach reminds us that not all agriculturalists look alike, and challenges various agrarian fundamentalist notions of farming as a benign enterprise, and all farmers as caretakers of the land (see Figure 3.3). In many countries, agriculture is a high-tech, capital-intensive, multi-billion dollar industry. The vested interest of farm

Police and agencies of the state	*Government laws and regulations related to land tenure, the environment, etc.*	*Pluriactivity/violations related to environmental regulations, labor laws, and other "crimes of the powerful"*	Offender
Social control			Criminal act
	Industrialization/ transformation of agriculture from local producers to integration within globalized commodity chains of production and distribution	*Ecological correlates and other factors which increase the attractiveness of farm property for theft and other crimes*	
The public			Victim

FIGURE 3.3 The square of crime: agricultural crime.

operators (and agricultural industries) to achieve efficiency and profit through various practices – from the use (and over-use) of farm chemicals and genetically modified organisms (Walters, 2004, 2006) to the pollution of water or wetlands with effluent from dairies, irrigated pastures, or grazing livestock (Barclay & Donnermeyer, 2007) – become part of a critical discourse on agricultural crime (Donnermeyer et al., 2011).

To be sure, there is plenty of room for other critical theories of agricultural crime and we are, by no means, claiming that left realism is the best or only way to explain this problem. Perspectives emerging from other new directions in critical criminology, such as eco-global criminology and green criminology (South & Brisman, 2013; White, 2011), will continue to inform critical rural criminological studies of agricultural crime. An intense critical dialogue about rural crime, law, and social control is a healthy way to develop a set of alternative explanations and policy implications to mainstream or orthodox versions of criminology, such as social disorganization theory (Donnermeyer, 2012).

Summary

In this chapter, we reviewed three topics related to rural crime. Our mission was two-fold. First, we wanted to review the extant rural literature. Second, we wanted to reinterpret the literature within a more critical framework. We used the square of crime to summarize the existing literature, to identify linkages of the micro and the macro, and to show possible avenues for future research. We admit that the square of crime may not be the best frame for all or any of the three topics. As well, we are not so pretentious as to strain the criminological imagination beyond credibility by claiming the square of crime is a general critical framework accounting for all factors, micro and macro, which would help us understand crime in the rural context. Further, we recognize that a diversity of critical criminology perspectives has not yet been applied to rural criminological issues, and we encourage others to apply their own frameworks, models, and theories. However, we have faith that this initial attempt will lead to other attempts to frame rural crime critically, first, so that the "numbers" found in the quantitative research do not display an undue amount of "magical objectivity," second, so that the more ethnographic, qualitative studies can be better contextualized by theory, and finally, so that comparative work on the rural can proceed in a more dynamic, intellectual milieu, where "conceptualization shifts" are most welcomed (Young, 2011, p. 55).

4

LOOKING FORWARD AND GLANCING BACK

Research, policy, and practice

> Much needs to be done to anticipate the needs and crime-related problems that will face rural America in the next few decades. Anticipating future problems, however, first requires a good understanding of the current state of affairs. Such an understanding is sorely lacking.
>
> *(Weisheit et al., 2006, pp. 180–181)*

The mission of this monograph was to articulate a critical rural criminology, which we first proposed several years ago (Donnermeyer & DeKeseredy, 2008). We attempted to accomplish this mission by confronting myths about crime in the rural context in Chapter 1, reviewing the origins of rural criminology and reprising previous critical work on violence against women in Chapter 2, and reframing three important areas of rural crime research from a more critical perspective in Chapter 3.

We also recognize that we ignored more issues about rural crime than the space allocated for this monograph could possibly include. Hence, our purpose in the first section of this final chapter is to briefly discuss five areas we did not cover in order to help emphasize the importance of future research and theory about rural crime, and to identify linkages between rural criminology and other specializations within criminology. We also observe that even this short list of areas does not cover all possible rural crime topics.

A second objective of this chapter is to discuss policy and practice from a critical point of view. Since the advent of left realism in the mid-1980s, the international critical criminological literature is ablaze with innovative policy proposals aimed at curbing crime in cities and suburbs. Needless to say, though, the question of what is to be done about law and order in rural communities has received very few answers. It is pointless to again carp about the selective inattention given to rural victims and perpetrators of crime because this does not move the field forward. Also, rural crime prevention and control are not totally ignored in progressive academic circles and several critical criminologists are working to advance a slew of policies designed to make rural communities safer.

Research

Environmental crime

Work on environmental crime is already a well-established body of literature and theory, and one of the fastest growing specializations within criminology (White, 2009; South & Brisman, 2013). Critical criminological perspectives have already profoundly aided its advancement (and vice versa), especially in the visibility and prominence of "green criminology," a major field of study in its own right within general criminology. As well, some of it overlaps with issues related to agriculture and crime (Walters, 2004, 2006), and with research about the impact of resource development on rural communities (Carrington et al., 2011; Wilkinson et al., 1984).

Rural criminology is fundamentally place-based in its approach to theory and research, and much of what is defined as environmental crime occurs at rural localities and affects rural people. Poaching (Forsyth, 2008: Muth, 1998) and violations of hunting and fishing regulations and harvesting quotas (Kuperan & Sutinen, 1998) are two areas where more rural work is needed, and land theft/land-grabbing, especially from Indigenous peoples by governments and corporate entities wishing to develop pristine areas for profits, is another (White, 2012). Illegal dumping, pollution, illegal logging, and other degradations of the environment by individuals and corporations pose on-going threats to the health and safety of all rural (and as well, urban) peoples (Clifford, 1998; Gunter & Kroll-Smith, 2007; Schmidt, 2009; Schriver & Kennedy,

2005; White, 2009). As well, illegal trafficking in flora and fauna has a clear rural dimension and shows how global networks of organized crime connect the rural and the urban.

Rural policing

At the present time, research on rural policing is mostly concentrated on rural Australia, Canada, Great Britain, and the U.S.A. Most of it is descriptive and a-theoretical (Donnermeyer et al., 2011; Jobes, 2002, 2003; Payne, Berg, & Sun, 2005; Weisheit et al., 2006), lacking any kind of critical perspective. Also, much of it has a tendency to veer off into pronouncements about the more "folksy" nature of rural policing styles, and if written by an author from the U.S.A., will inevitably make reference to the iconic 1960s TV program, *The Andy Griffith Show*, and the warm-hearted adventures of Sheriff Andy Taylor and the inept but likeable Deputy Barney Fife, in the quaint, small town of Mayberry, the epitome of a *Gemeinschaft* idyll. Not only is there a dearth of comparative studies across differing kinds of rural communities, there are no studies which have attempted to link the interplay of policing within the context of rural structure and culture. Simply put, the studies are either of single locations or are empirically based surveys of multiple rural agencies on such mundane criminological phenomena as policing styles (e.g., traditional enforcement versus community-oriented policing or the more generalist nature of rural police).

Unfortunately, what is left out are the ways rural policing styles are embedded in social and economic structures that define the distinctive features of enforcement, given the diversity of rural communities and people (Kraska & Cubellis, 1997). Research on variations in the ways police differentially enforce laws and conduct themselves with citizens (both criminals and law-abiding members) would provide valuable insights for critical criminological theories of policing, and for the development of appropriate strategies, given the geographic size of rural jurisdictions and the relatively small number of police personnel in most rural police agencies (Jobes, 2003; Weisheit et al., 2006).

One way to blaze new trails for the critical criminological study of policing is to adopt a definition of a local jurisdiction in the rural context in a way similar to the definition of a community by Liepins (2000). In her words, "an approach to community must determine a way in which the population involved can be treated as a set of heterogeneous figures who constantly locate themselves in multiple positions and groups" (p. 29). Hence, communities are "temporally and locationally specific terrains of power and discourse" (p. 29). Within these rural communities are various kinds of social orders that interplay with the formal structures of policing to define responses to differing kinds of offenses, from intimate violence against women to agricultural crime.

Without connecting the specifics to these larger structures and processes, understanding policing in the rural context will continue down a road of testing specific actions without ever considering macro-level forces that place strong parameters on the ways in which rural communities, peoples, and police agencies interact in the present and can change in the future to create more effective partnerships (Donnermeyer et al., 2011).

Rural others

A pioneering book, and one that greatly helped the development of rural criminology, is the reader by Neil Chakraborti and Jon Garland (2004) titled *Rural Racism*. Focused on the rural sector of Great Britain, the chapters on race and hate groups speak volumes about the same issues in most other societies around the world. Examining hate groups, many of which have rural roots and mostly act out their biases in rural environments (Dees & Fiffer, 2001; Kimmel & Ferber, 2000; Turk, 2004; van Dyke & Soule, 2002; Young, 1990), is a vital arena for rural criminological research and theorizing. For example, in the U.S.A. alone, according to the Southern Poverty Law Center (2011), there are now over 1,000 identifiable hate groups, ranging from traditional chapters of the Ku Klux Klan to branches of a racist right-wing religious group known as Christian Identity, with a disproportionate share of all hate groups located in rural areas.

Also important about the Chakraborti and Garland (2004) book is the fact that they bring into the study of rural criminology a perspective that considers geography from a critical focus, where power, inequality, segmentation, multiple expressions of collective efficacy, and localized forms of macro-level change are played out in a arena that can be understood in terms of a host of crime-related issues (Cloke & Little, 1997; Hogg & Carrington, 2003). As we mention later, there is much to be done in research, policy, and practice on the plight of Indigenous peoples in many parts of the world (Cowlishaw, 2013; Cunneen, 2001, 2007; Wood, 2009), which is an issue also related to studies of rural policing styles.

In this book, we have advocated for re-creating older functionalist renditions of an ecological approach in criminology into a critical version of the same. Research focused on marginalized and minority groups by race, ethnicity, gay and lesbian lifestyles, religious sects, and unique subcultures, among others, helps us to understand how rural social structure and culture contextualizes issues related to crime, safety, and policing (Hogg & Carrington, 2006).

Interpersonal violence: beyond violence against women

DeKeseredy (2011b) and others are pioneers in the advancement of a critical rural criminology through their focus on the localized contexts in which women are the victims of violence by their intimate partners. They extended their work beyond the city because their critical perspective helped them see with more than an urban-centric lens of misplaced dichotomies. Their work serves to remind criminology scholars that the rural sectors of many societies have a disproportionate share of other vulnerable populations, including the elderly and children. Forms of domestic violence extend to consideration of their situations, and the same critical approach to the study of child abuse (Vieth, 1998–1999) and elder abuse (National Research Council, 2003) in the rural context should follow the lead of research on violence against women. Some forms of abuse against children and the elderly (Cupitt, 1997; Dimah & Dimah, 2004), as well as women, may be associated with addictions and the need to support drug dependency (Haight et al., 2005). Hence, once again, we note that the crime issues confronting rural peoples and communities around the world are intertwined in a tightly knit quilt of micro- and macro-level factors.

As mentioned briefly in Chapter 3, some rural work has been completed on the "subculture of violence" (Lee, 2008; Nisbett, 1993), with the focus on the unique cultural features of a wide region, such as the southern and western states of the U.S.A. Frequently, work in this area has focused on cultural features of a region which are undeniably rural, seeking to link these characteristics to variations in crime. Some of this may be an artifact of a region's history of economic and social development that leaves behind cultural echoes expressed by social relations in contemporary times (Nisbett & Cohen, 1996), even though such claims are difficult to prove (Chu, Rivera, & Loftin, 2000) Although this kind of analysis is fraught with conceptual traps associated with the ecological fallacy (Robinson, 1950), it is worth noting that additional research using a critical perspective, such as the square of crime, has the potential to untangle some of the threads about how forms of collective efficacy in rural localities create criminogenic conditions.

Synergies and comparisons

The rural crime literature is surprisingly large, especially scholarly work published since 1990, once an interested scholar takes the time to look. Admittedly, the volume is not nearly as great as the deluge of urban-based studies, most of which do not really consider urban contexts because they are merely pieces of narrowly focused abstracted empiricism whose data happened to be collected in a city or cities. One possible problem with the lower volume of rural-focused studies is that submissions with data based on rural peoples and rural communities find it harder to be published in mainstream journals.[1] Another is that, until recently, there has been no place to publish explicitly rural work. However, the recent development of the *International Journal of Rural Criminology* is a hopeful first step in providing a home for a cadre of high-quality rural-based criminological research.[2]

Beyond the valuable contributions of edited books (Barclay, Donnermeyer, Scott, & Hogg, 2007; Carter et al., 1982; Chakraborti & Garland, 2004; Dingwall & Moody, 1999; Edwards, 1992; Mawby & Yarwood, 2011; Robertson, Sloboda, Boyd, Beatty, & Kozel, 1997), special issue of journals (Edwards & Donnermeyer, 2002; Phillips & Hundersmarck, 2008), and monographs (DeKeseredy & Schwartz, 2009; Garriott, 2011; Hogg & Carrington, 2006; O'Connor & Gray, 1989; Websdale, 1998; Weisheit et al., 2006), there are two greater needs to be met if rural crime scholarship is to advance. They are: (1) a need for more comparative work across diverse rural places, achieved through rigorous designs of both qualitatively and quantitatively oriented studies which are informed by theory and concepts (Young, 2011); and (2) a need for more scholarly work which attempts to review and synthesize the already existing literature. Either way, it is time to push the boundaries of rural work beyond a few countries which dominate the extant literature, namely, Australia, Canada, Great Britain, and the United States, and the handful of topics discussed in this monograph.

Fully 49% of the world is rural, and searching about, looking for more obscure published research from other countries, like those proverbial "needles in a haystack," is greatly needed. For example, a surprising number of studies about violence against women can be found in the journal *World Development*, a journal focused on development in societies across the globe and on the improvement of peoples' living conditions. Hence, it includes the occasional peer-reviewed research about the relationship of a crime which affects the changing status of women in many developing societies in regard to their quality of life.

With "tongues in cheek," we note that the field of criminology is highly segmented, with various divisions, sub-disciplines, and sub-specializations within the sub-disciplines – hardly the stuff of collective efficacy. A great deal of this research represents forms of horizontal knowledge (Bernstein, 2000) through the endless retesting of data with new methodological twists and turns that do little to advance knowledge, and the development of overly specialized theories, pint-size in scope, which add jargon but little else (except more paper sessions at the American Society of Criminology annual meeting). Rural criminology is one area whose development is young enough that this need not occur. The use of critical criminological perspectives, especially those which can help define a critical ecological/geographic approach to rural criminology, which can stand in counter-distinction to the functionalist version which continues to underpin ecological approaches which evolved out of the Chicago School of sociology, and which accounts for both micro- and macro-level social forces, has the potential to provide a substantial amount of scholarly unity to the field, while still allowing for a plurality of perspectives to examine diverse criminological issues across the gamut of rural places around the world.

Policy and practice

Scholarship is useless without implications for policy and practice. In this section, we suggest ways policy and practice can help build safer rural environments.

Stricter gun control

This chapter was written shortly after one of the worst mass killings in U.S. history. The horrific event took place on December 14, 2012, in Newtown, Connecticut, leaving 20 schoolchildren and eight adults dead. The killer, 20-year-old Adam Lanza, was fully armed and wore earplugs to shut out the screams of his victims at Sandy Hook Elementary School while he fired 150 rounds from a Bushmaster AR-15 assault rifle. He killed himself after the slaughter and the motives for his actions remain unclear (Atkins, 2013). Millions of people around the world know the gruesome details of Lanza's killing spree, but it is safe to assume that most of them do not know that the rural, hilly areas near Sandy Hook are riddled with unlicensed gun ranges that routinely attract owners of automatic weapons. *New York Times* reporters Michael Moss and Ray Rivera (2012, p. 7) offer a more detailed description of this problem in Box 4.1.

Box 4.1 Guns were part of a town that is full of pain

"Something needs to be done," said Joel T. Faxon, a hunter and a member of the town's police commission, who championed ... restrictions.

> These are not normal guns that people need. These are guns for an arsenal, and you get lunatics like this guy who goes into a school fully armed and protected to take return fire. We live in a town, not in a war.

"It was like this continuous, rapid fire," said Amy Habboush, who became alarmed last year when she heard what sounded like machine guns, although she did not call the police. "We knew there was target practice, but we hadn't heard that noise before."

Earlier this year, the Newtown police chief, Michael Kehoe, went to the Town Council for help. The town had a 20-year-old ordinance aimed at hunters that included a ban on shooting within 150 meters of occupied dwellings, but the chief complained that the way the law was written had left him powerless to enforce the rules.

The police logged more than 50 gunfire complaints this year through July, double the number for all of 2011....

Mr. Faxon, who is a lawyer, said he wrote the ordinance, which would have imposed more constraints on shooting, including limited hours, and a requirement that any target shooting range, and the firearms used there be approved by the chief of police.

The proposal was submitted to the council's ordinance committee, whose chairwoman, Mary Ann Jacob, would play a heroic role in the shooting. Ms. Jacob is a librarian aide at Sandy Hook Elementary School, where she is credited with protecting many lives by throwing two rooms crowded with children into lockdown as the gunfire erupted.

"We're growing," Ms. Jacob said, describing a town where hikers and mountain bikers compete with gun owners for the use of many trails and wooded areas.

After two meetings, and an outpouring of opposition, the proposed ordinance was put on hold.

The explosions his neighbors hear are targets that are legally available at hunting outlets, said Scott Ostrosky, the owner of an informal gun range. "If you're good old boys like we are, they are exciting," he said.

Mr. Ostrosky said guns should not be made the "scapegoat" in the school massacre. "Guns are why we're free in this country, and people lose sight of that when tragedies like this happen," he said. "A gun didn't kill all those children, a disturbed man killed all those children."

The Newtown mass murder sparked another fierce debate about gun control in a country with an "abundance of firearms" (Currie, 1985), and there are millions of people who support claims such as those made by Mr. Ostrosky in Box 4.1. However, he is undeniably wrong in stating that Adam Lanza's violent acts constitute a "tragedy." Rather, his violent behavior was outright criminal, all too common in the U.S.A., and preventable. Furthermore, all countries have "lunatics," but unlike a sizeable portion of U.S. citizens, most residents of other countries around the world are not "armed to the teeth" (Reiman & Leighton, 2010). In fact, with less than 5% of the world's population, the U.S.A. is home to between 35% and 50% of the world's civilian-owned firearms. To make matters worse, the U.S.A. has the world's highest rate of gun ownership, with an average of 88 per 100 people. The U.S.A. also ranks number 28 in the world's firearm murder rate (2.97 per 100,000 people) (Rogers, 2012). Yet, a recent review of two nationally representative surveys by the Pew Research Center for the People & the Press (2013) indicates that the actual percentage of American households who have a gun in their homes has not only not gone up, but has actually declined since 1970, based on results from the General Social Survey and the Gallup Organization. Despite this, guns sales have increased (Horwitz, 2013). We suggest that these two seemingly contradictory facts can be reconciled if persons in households where there are guns already are buying more in anticipation of stricter gun control laws, and perhaps even stockpiling weapons to protect themselves from various perceived threats.

Contrary to popular belief, in the U.S.A. and Canada, two countries which consistently rank relatively high, internationally, in homicide rates (Currie, 1985, 2009), rural areas have higher rates of gun ownership than urban and metropolitan places. Not surprisingly, many rural gun owners hunt wildlife and own rifles, but the rate of rural handgun ownership is also higher than that for cities. Some scholars estimate that the rural rate in the U.S.A. is at least 8% greater (Weisheit et al., 2006), while the most recent Canadian statistics show that 37.3% of small town residents own a gun compared to 2.8% in communities with over one million people (Department of Justice Canada, 2013). Additionally, in Canada, close to 50% of domestic homicides involving firearms occurred in rural communities, though rural homes account for less than 20% of

Canada's population (Royal Canadian Mounted Police, 2013; World Bank, 2013).

Suffice it to say, eliminating firearms altogether will not alone reduce the rates of rural violence described in Chapter 1 and elsewhere. Likewise, strict firearms abolition in cities does not guarantee that urban places devastated by high levels of poverty and unemployment will not be damaged by violence. As Currie (2009) puts it in his commentary on violent crime in the U.SA.: "In the real world, the United States is awash in guns, and the prevalence of guns cannot be separated from other aspects of American culture and social policy that have contributed to the country's unusually high level of violence" (p. 110). For this and other reasons, critical criminologists contend that progressives need to constantly focus on solutions that target social and economic exclusion. Nevertheless, stricter regulation of guns does help save lives. For example, in Australia in 1996, certain rapid-fire long guns were banned under the National Firearms Agreement. This legislation led to the buyback of 650,000 guns and to stricter rules for licensing and safe storage. The law did not end gun ownership, but the murder rate with firearms has now dropped by more than 40% and the suicide rate with firearms has dropped by more than 50% (Kristof, 2012).

The answer, then, is not to ban all guns, but to craft better safety standards such as eliminating easy access to handguns and rapid-firing assault rifles. In the words of Reiman and Leighton (2010),

> Trying to fight crime while allowing such easy access to guns is like trying to teach a child to walk and then tripping him each time he stands up. In its most charitable light, it is hypocrisy. Less charitably, it is complicity in murder.
>
> *(p. 201)*

Ironically, toy guns are regulated in the U.S.A., but real ones are not as carefully controlled. Indeed, it is time for change and on top of eliminating easy access to guns, U.S. politicians should carefully examine the following proposals suggested by Kristof (2012, p. 15):

- Limit gun purchases to one a month.
- Restrict the sale of high-capacity magazines.

- Impose a universal background check for gun buyers, even with private sales.
- Make serial numbers difficult to erase and support California in its attempt to require that new handguns imprint a micro-stamp on each shell so that it can be traced back to a particular gun.

Progressive scholars and activists in countries with liberal gun laws must team up and lobby policy-makers for stricter gun regulations. After all, as Kristof reminds us, there are strict regulations for things such as ladders which kill far fewer people than do guns. Hopefully, street-level protests, the use of social media (e.g., Facebook and Twitter), and other collective efforts will make stricter gun control much more than a "thought experiment" (Currie, 2009).

Creating meaningful employment

Perhaps no one states this better than Elliott Currie (2013): "We need to think about making meaningful and sustaining work a human right, much as health care is in most of the advanced societies" (p. 14). Certainly, throughout the world, an alarming number of rural people are living "at the razor's edge" (Jensen, 2006). Recall the data on Louisiana, Mississippi, and Alabama presented in Chapter 2. One of the key reasons for high rural unemployment is industrial restructuring that reduces jobs, which is related to a variety of crimes (DeKeseredy & Schwartz, 2009). And, there is a uniqueness to rural unemployment. For example, self-employment and farming are major rural occupations in the U.S.A. that often do not qualify for unemployment compensation. As well, in scores of rural areas, compared to their urban counterparts, rural jobless people have to travel very long distances to employment offices and this requires a greater expenditure of limited resources (Tigges & Fuguitt, 2003).

What is to be done? More government funds should be devoted to industrial and agricultural development and to job training. Moreover, government tax incentives should be given to companies to entice them to locate in rural communities. Such enticements, though, should only be given to corporations that sincerely commit to giving workers a decent wage. Consider what Caterpillar Inc. recently did in Canada with federal government assistance, described in Box 4.2 by Laurel MacDowell (2012, pp. 1–2). What is not mentioned there, however, is that this company did eventually close the London, Ontario, plant in February, 2012 and created new jobs at a plant in Muncie, Indiana, which pay half as much as the unionized workers in London received.

Box 4.2 What's wrong with Caterpillar?

Local 27 members of the Canadian Auto Workers (CAW) union were locked out on New Year's Day by Caterpillar Inc.'s Electro-Motive Diesel in a callous display of corporate might, by a company that may be intending to leave Canada.

On December 27, 2011, plant workers rejected an offer that would have cut wages to less than half; eliminated a pension plan, and cut other benefits in half. A skilled worker making $35 an hour would, under this new proposal, receive $16.50 an hour. The current minimum wage in Ontario, for 2011, is $10.25 per hour. These employees have families, mortgages and households like other Canadians, so the wages offered are not living wages.

The federal government is certainly involved with Caterpillar and not neutral. On March 19, 2008, Prime Minister Harper visited the Electro-Motive plant to showcase a $5 million federal tax break for buyers of the diesel locomotive-maker's wares and a wider $1 billion tax break on industrial capital investment. Yet, Caterpillar has received attention, since the 1990s, as a terrible employer with a very regressive business culture. If our political culture were guided by ethics, our government would not offer incentives to this company. It would judge them unfit to operate in this country and, instead, encourage a local, Canadian, ethical competitor, if one existed, or encourage competition in that sector.

After this company received the government go-ahead to purchase, and a large tax break, it treated these Canadian workers with total disrespect. To add insult to injury, its attempt to extract unreasonable wage and benefit concessions from Canadian union members is likely an excuse to shift production of electric-powered diesel engines and associated railroad components to a start-up and lower-wage plant in Muncie, Indiana. There, the company has received lucrative incentives (more public money) from Indiana's anti-union state government for the Muncie start-up. There, it advertised for a Human Resources manager with the stipulation that he/she have "experience with providing union-free culture and union avoidance."

For many readers, Box 4.2 probably triggers memories of reading the roots of rural critical criminology in Chapter 2. Based on the actions of Caterpillar Inc. and other greedy corporations, and the rapidly increasing gap between the "haves and the have-nots," most critical criminologists such as Rick Matthews (2012) would strongly agree with Russell's (2002) assertion that "Marxism remains as relevant as ever for analyzing crime, criminal justice and the role of the state" (p. 113). Furthermore, Box 4.2 is likely to influence many left-wing scholars and activists to revisit this left realist policy advanced 30 years ago by Raymond Michalowski (1983):

> The passage of local tax initiatives to establish a tax surcharge on any industry to close plants or permanently reduce the work force in that community. The objective would be to assess industries for a certain period of time (e.g., three years) in order to offset the real costs imposed upon the community by plant relocation or work force reduction: the payment of additional unemployment benefits, the retraining of local workers, and the loss of revenue due to a decline of property values.
>
> *(p. 15)*

While few in number, there are companies with a stronger business ethic than Caterpillar Inc. and other anti-union corporations (Clinard & Yeager, 1980). DeKeseredy and Schwartz (2009) are two rural critical criminologists who argue that such companies should be strongly encouraged to contribute to ongoing efforts to curb rural poverty and unemployment and their devastating consequences. One way businesses can achieve this goal is by helping to build a more diverse rural economy through developing and supporting small, community-based businesses and small industrial districts. These incentives can be created with small business loans, ethical tax incentives, and government–private sector partnerships (Jensen, 2006).

It is unclear whether he still holds this view, but 30 years ago Michalowski (1983) sharply disagreed with the notion of government support for jobs suggested by us and DeKeseredy and Schwartz (2009). As he put it then,

> Attempts to utilize state power to create full employment must avoid traditional liberal traps of creating costly programs which, since they are largely financed by income taxes on the wages of worker rather than taxes on corporate profits, ultimately create intra-class conflicts between the employed and the unemployed/ underemployed segments of the working-class.
>
> *(p. 17)*

Is there a progressive alternative? Michalowski's answered this question with a resounding "yes!" For him, superior alternatives informed by thinking critically about crime are publicly run, non-profit corporations that provide jobs for unemployed people and whose key objectives are to perform useful services to the communities in which they are based and to society in general. The following are Michalowski's examples of such services which are not profitable enough for private sector corporations and that are not normally deemed state responsibilities:

- retrofitting government buildings with energy-saving devices;
- producing a variety of entertainments and arts;[3]
- reclaiming land;
- recycling non-renewable and renewable resources; and
- building and maintaining an adequate supply of public bathrooms in all American cities.

(p. 17)

There is a famous scene in the 1996 Hollywood movie *Jerry Maguire* where actors Cuba Gooding Jr. and Tom Cruise yell "Show me the money" over their phones during a conversation with each other. Indeed, where will the financial support for the above initiatives come from? According to Michalowski, funds will be partially derived from a corporate unemployment tax indexed to the rate of unemployment. He claims that this approach is a more "dignified" alternative to the degradation ceremonies[4] associated with receiving the current form of unemployment insurance. He also asserts that this tax would provide corporations with a greater incentive to reduce unemployment. For criminologists and those who have been victimized by crime, another important outcome of Michalowski's solution is that it "would reduce the number of people for whom crime appeared to be a reasonable emotional or instrumental alternative to the goals of achieving egoistic self-identity and material adequacy" (p. 18).

Michalowski's model is an important step toward creating what Currie (2013) refers to as a "sustaining society." However, in this day and age of the U.S. "fiscal cliff,"[5] "turbo-charged capitalism" (Luttwak, 1995), intense government and corporate assaults on collective bargaining, and a host of other major problems caused by free-market capitalism, it is highly unlikely that we will see it come to fruition in the near future. When, then, will it happen? Maybe Michalowski is right to assert that:

> It is when people begin to take charge of their own existence through collective action that the outer perimeter of capitalist ideology which protects the deeper structure of class formation will begin to erode, laying the groundwork for fundamental, structural change in American society.
>
> *(1983, p. 22)*

Michalowski's made this statement 30 years ago and things have only gotten worse for the working class in rural and urban communities. Still, it can't be emphasized enough that regardless of when the above transformation occurs, crime in rural areas (and in urban ones) cannot be effectively curbed without the provision of quality jobs. Furthermore, creating such employment reduces inequality, which, as is demonstrated in countries like Japan, Austria, and Finland, results in widespread economic growth and superior results in health, education, life expectancy, and productivity (Brennan & Stamford, 2012; Wilkinson & Pickett, 2009).

Reducing woman abuse[6]

Job training and education

As stated in Chapter 1 and other sources (e.g., DeKeseredy & Schwartz, 2009; Rennison et al., 2012, in press), woman abuse is a major problem in rural communities, one that can also be reduced with full and decent employment (DeKeseredy, Alvi, Schwartz, & Tomaszewski, 2003; Renzetti, 2011). Related to this solution is the need for policy-makers to support more job training and education. These initiatives help battered women find work and eventually achieve financial security and independence (DeKeseredy, 2011b; Purdon, 2003). Still, government agencies should not assume that all women who get jobs as a result of state-sponsored job training and education programs will automatically be safe. For instance, there is a large empirical literature showing that some current and former male partners engage in "patriarchal terrorism" at women's workplaces (Johnson, 1995). In other words, these men stalk and harass women at work, and some men have killed women in the workplace (Renzetti, 2011; Sokoloff & Dupont, 2005).

Often, too, violent means of "sabotaging work efforts" influence employers to fire women to avoid problems in the workplace and to protect coworkers (Conlin, Chapman, & Bensen, 2006). Thus, it is crucial that policies be created that guarantee abused women the ability to collect unemployment insurance if they cannot work due to injuries sustained from their current or ex-partners' abusive behaviors. Legislation is also necessary to prohibit employers from firing women who are being stalked or assaulted at work (Brandwein, 1999; DeKeseredy & Schwartz, 2009).

On top of economically excluded rural women being ensured quality jobs, they should, like all women, receive equal pay for equal work. In the U.S.A., for example, women's earnings are between 70% and 77% those of men (Catalyst, 2012), and as described in Box 4.3 (Brennan, 2012), economic equality for Canadian women is "centuries off." This is blatant discrimination, and if more women had jobs paying them decent wages, there would be fewer on social assistance and in battered women's shelters. Further, more women would work if they had access to affordable, quality childcare (Cancian & Danziger, 2009; Renzetti, 2011).

Box 4.3 Economic equality for women still centuries off: parity won't occur until year 2593, study shows

Given the global pace of economic change for women in Canada, they should not expect to enjoy real equality for another six centuries, a Queen's University[7] law professor says.

Taking into account a number of factors from 1997 until present time, Kathleen Lahey has determined that women will not be celebrating Women's Equality Day until 2593 – or 581 years from now.

"Because women do over half the unpaid work in Canada and do nearly half of the paid work in Canada, economic parity is a long way away. And the rate of change has been virtually non-existent since 1997," Lahey said Tuesday.

"It's not good," she said, adding that she hopes the calculation in her study proves to be wrong.

Lahey said the recession of the early 1990s and the most recent recession erased many of the gains women had made from 1977 to 1993, noting that they benefitted little from billions of dollars in federal and provincial infrastructure spending.

"The progress that women had experienced came to an absolute standstill in 1997. It did not even change by a fraction of a percentage point from 1997 to 2010," she said.

She said from 2008 to the end of this fiscal year, Ottawa will have spent $168 billion on major changes in tax structure, infrastructure spending programs and employment insurance programs – all of which give the bulk of benefits to men.

Lahey said the 2012 budget changes to Canada's Old Age Security and Guaranteed Income Supplement, health-care spending, the national private retirement system, infrastructure spending and public services and employment will impose the heaviest cuts on women and members of other vulnerable groups.

"There are a lot of different factors that influence the status of women. It is a very complex process but the bottom line is that most of the things in both public spending and the tax system tend

> to reflect market status. And, as long as women are under-represented in terms of market income, they will receive less when it comes to any tax cuts, spending change or whatever, whereas spending cuts will hit them usually quite quickly," she said.

Job training and education will also prevent many men for engaging in woman abuse. For example, rural men who lost their farms or jobs in industries such as shoe manufacturing would be much less likely to spend time drinking or doing drugs with their friends if they were given the opportunity to achieve meaningful and adequately remunerative employment. Hence, their relationships would more likely remain intact, they would be less likely to receive patriarchal peer support such as that described in Chapter 2, and they would be much less likely to abuse women as an attempt to repair damage to their male identity (DeKeseredy & Schwartz, 2009).

Confronting pornography

New electronic technologies are emerging everywhere and are part and parcel of a rapidly growing number of people's lives. What Walter DeKeseredy and Martin Schwartz (2013) state in their book on patriarchal male peer support should be repeated here: Count yourself very fortunate or lucky if you are reading this chapter without being periodically interrupted by electronic mail, cell phone text messages, and/or phone calls. This is not to say that these and other new means of electronic communication do not have many advantages. They definitely do, but, as described in Chapter 1, new technologies also have many destructive features that harm millions of women and children. Pornography is one in particular that stands out and it is a powerful correlate of woman abuse regardless of whether it takes place in rural, suburban, or urban communities.

DeKeseredy and Schwartz (2013) are among a growing number of anti-pornography scholars who assert that an effective way of challenging pornography is to boycott companies and services that disseminate pornographic materials like those described in Chapter 1. For them, and others, this is a vital component of a multi-pronged approach to curbing woman abuse. As well, boycotting makes a difference because of its financial impact. Even so, as DeKeseredy and Schwartz point out, boycotting is most effective when it is combined with social media protests on Twitter, Facebook, and the like.

Boycotting is a daunting task because sexism is all around us. Of course, too, there is never enough time in the day to monitor the myriad ways in which women are objectified, dehumanized, and exploited on the Internet and in other media. Given their work, family, and other commitments, people must carefully pick their battles. Even so, new technologies make it much easier than it was in the past to collectively expose and criticize hurtful media coverage of woman abuse and to boycott companies that profit from misogyny (DeKeseredy & Schwartz, 2013).

Second generation crime prevention through environmental design (CPTED)[8]

As noted by Saville (2004), "There is this persistent belief that CPTED ends at the physical environment; that our responsibility stops by modifying the built environment to reduce crime opportunities" (p. 1). Further, CPTED in its original form focused mainly on curbing public crimes in socially and economically disenfranchised urban communities, such as improving the territorial control people have over their buildings (DeKeseredy et al., 2003), and it ignored private crimes, such as violence against women (DeKeseredy, Alvi, Renzetti, & Schwartz, 2004). As well, there were concerns that the first generation of CPTED merely displaced crime and that demographic, economic, sociological, and cultural features of place were far more predictive of crime and criminal opportunities than a locality's physical dimensions (Brassard, 2003; Cozens, Saville, & Hillier, 2005).

Reacting to these pitfalls, some criminologists have crafted a second generation CPTED, one that focuses heavily on generating the kinds of collective efficacy through community capacity building that can act as a counterforce to rural patriarchy and other forms of rural social organization that perpetuate and legitimate woman abuse (Cleveland & Saville, 2003; DeKeseredy et al., 2009). Second generation CPTED is similar in some way to the concept of *community readiness* (Donnermeyer et al., 1997; Edwards, Jumper-Thurman, Plested, Oetting, & Swanson,

2000). The idea of readiness is that there are levels or stages of support for localized interventions and preventive actions among neighborhood and community leaders. Actions that enhance the readiness of local leaders/elites to take woman abuse seriously are key to building positive forms of collective efficacy and strengthening specific actions among all citizens (both leaders and followers) that may be undertaken to reduce woman abuse in its many shapes and forms.

Second generation CPTED is about developing and improving types of defensible space through engaging in community level activities that create forms of locality-based discourses concerning norms, beliefs, and values about security issues which can function to deter potential offenders (Cleveland & Saville, 2003; Saville, 2004). It is grounded in Liepins (2000) concept of a community as a place where power and inequality are expressed on a daily basis (Jobes et al., 2005), but with the potential to change as practices/behaviors and associated meanings (beliefs and values) are changed. We argue, therefore, that another way to construct a critical approach to the ecology of crime is to base both policy and practice on a firm theoretical base about what is realistically possible within community contexts and among networks of people/actors at the local level.

Here, following our earlier work (see DeKeseredy et al., 2009), we focus on rural communities and the idea that rural patriarchy, as a harmful variant of collective efficacy, may be diminished and even eliminated through appropriate activities that strengthen other forms of collective efficacy which enhance the security of rural women and deter abusive/violent behavior by rural men. Note that DeKeseredy et al. (2004) have already provided examples of how these strategies informed by a gendered second generation CPTED, can be modified to help reduce private violence against women in North American urban public housing.

One key element of second generation CPTED is the development of new versions of a community's culture, which can be accomplished through the development and/or re-creation of a "shared history" through the use of festivals, sporting events, music, and art (Cleveland & Saville, 2003). Occasionally defined as "placemaking" (Adams & Goldbard, 2001), this initiative involves the use of plays, concerts, and paintings that sensitize rural residents to the harms caused by woman abuse. Such cultural work, including designing tee shirts and quilts to memorialize women's victimization, could be done in schools, places of worship, county fairs, community centers, and other visible places with the assistance of community members. This type of cultural work is routinely done in many parts of Ohio, which is deemed to be "a Mecca for the quilt community" (Feldman, 2004, p. 4).

Although the activities may appear mundane and old-fashioned, perhaps even trivial, their revised context represents one set of strategies for breaking down rural patriarchy and promoting greater awareness of woman abuse by giving public voice to the issue and confronting public expressions of rural patriarchy. They also serve to increase the readiness of communities to sustain actions on a wider scale (Donnermeyer et al., 1997), supported by law enforcement, elected officials, and other local elites, because it is expedient and in their vested interest to conform to new standards, rather than clinging tightly to anachronistic forms of patriarchy.

Another key element of second generation CPTED is development of connectivity and a pro-feminist masculinity. Abused rural women suffer from higher levels of social and geographic isolation than their urban counterparts (DeKeseredy & Schwartz, 2009; Logan, Stevenson, Evans, & Leukefeld, 2004; Rennison et al., in press). Therefore, it is necessary to build easily accessible women's centers in rural communities or very close to them (Hornosty & Doherty, 2002). The creation of these safe places should be done with private and public support, and they do not have to focus only on issues related to abuse. For example, with the assistance of U.S. Department of Labor demonstration grants, similar to job readiness programs offered in Kentucky woman abuse shelters,[9] women's centers could offer educational programs aimed at training unemployed women for jobs contributing to their economic independence. These centers would also be the locus for artistic events and other social activities, as well as providing childcare, to give women time to seek jobs or to get a brief reprieve from the pressures of childrearing

Apart from providing supportive spaces for women to connect, we need to encourage greater connection among the many men eager to eliminate woman abuse. That we are increasingly seeing "the presence of alternative masculinities incompatible with violence in rural communities" offers hope that "large-scale transformations in the rural gender order are possible over time that may in turn lead to reductions in gendered violence" (Hogg & Carrington, 2006, p. 183). Even so, regardless of where they live, most anti-sexist men do not have opportunities to socialize with other males who are concerned about enhancing women's safety. Thus, formal pro-feminist men's organizations, such as the National Organization of Men Against Sexism and the White Ribbon Campaign should be invited to hold town hall meetings in community centers and other settings where pro-feminist men can get together and develop individual and collective strategies to reduce woman abuse.

A general point of agreement in the international pro-feminist men's movement is that men must take an active role in stopping woman abuse and eliminating other forms of patriarchal control and domination throughout society. Moreover, pro-feminist men place the responsibility for woman abuse squarely on abusive men. A widely cited assertion is that "since it is men who are the offenders, it should be men – not women – who change their behavior (Thorne-Finch, 1992, p. 236). As well, pro-feminist men strongly adhere to the notion that "as fathers, friends, lovers, husbands, and colleagues, *all men* have a stake in putting an end to violence against women" (Sev'er, 2012, p. 94, emphasis in original).

Much more can be said about the philosophy, political beliefs, and history of the pro-feminist men's movement, but it is beyond the scope of this book to reproduce this information here. Similarly, there is now a relatively large literature on the many things men can do individually or collectively to end gendered violence that we urge readers to examine.[10] Below are few examples of pro-feminist men's strategies that can be implemented in rural areas and elsewhere:

- protesting and boycotting strip clubs, bars with live sex shows, hotels that rent pornographic videos, and "adult stores" such as the Lion's Den (see Chapter 1) that rent or sell pornography;
- confronting men who make sexist jokes and who abuse their female partners;
- supporting and participating in woman abuse awareness programs; and

- expressing their views by supporting and voting for local officials with similar beliefs and who are ready and willing to implement policies and actions that breakdown rural patriarchy related to violence against women (DeKeseredy et al., 2009; DeKeseredy & Schwartz, 2013; Funk, 2006; Katz, 2006).

Men's groups can also discuss how and where male members can apply for jobs, effective job interview strategies, and ideas for opening or running a small business (DeKeseredy et al., 2004). Initiatives such as these, and those listed above, according to proponents of second generation CPTED, bring people together "in common purpose" and connect them with outside groups that can help them acquire financial and other forms of support for their peacemaking efforts. Outside groups, such as the Ohio Domestic Violence Network, also help people avoid reinventing the wheel (Thorne-Finch, 1992). For example, established women's groups and male anti-sexist collectives located in other rural communities can offer existing sets of best practices that can be tailored to meet their needs and be quickly implemented at little or no financial cost. Nevertheless, regardless of which strategies are suggested, as Logan et al. (2004) correctly point out, "creative solutions must be developed in order to serve women with victimization histories within the context of the specific communities where these women live" (p. 58).

The third element in a second generation CPTED is addressing issues related to fear of crime. Fear of crime is increased in rural communities by low levels of policing, the absence of streetlighting, and other factors (Weisheit et al., 2006). As in North American public housing estates, vandalism is a powerful determinant of women's fear of crime in rural areas (DeKeseredy et al., 2009; Donnermeyer & Phillips, 1984).[11] Such fear influences many women to stay indoors, which makes it even more difficult for them to obtain knowledge about services available to abused women and to develop social ties with neighbors who might be willing to confront the men who assault them in their homes or elsewhere (DeKeseredy & MacLeod, 1997; DeKeseredy & Schwartz, 2009).

Note that a key finding of Sampson et al.'s (1998) study of collective efficacy, despite their one-dimensional interpretation of the concept, is that community threshold can be enhanced and violent crimes can be reduced in neighborhoods of concentrated urban disadvantage when people band together for informal social control and to pool their collective power to extract such resources as garbage collection and housing code enforcement. Saville (1996) also recognizes "tipping points": that is, places are composed of people and groups with a capacity for action that is not unlimited. In terms of informal social control within contested communities, actions taken through a gendered second generation CPTED help tip the balance in favor of pro-feminist approaches. As well, these activities have positive, ancillary benefits when they are publicly visible, by symbolically declaring that woman abuse is wrong and has no place in a rural community, hence, increasing the readiness of community leaders by putting pressure on them to support interventions that reduce woman abuse, and connecting it to their vested interest to be re-elected and/or reappointed (Donnermeyer et al., 1997).

Second generation CPTED studies show that teaching positive communication skills and conflict resolution enhances community cohesiveness (Gilligan, 2001; Saville & Clear, 2000). To reduce woman abuse in it myriad forms, then, rural schools (as well as urban ones) should build empathy into the curriculum through constant attention to the intersections of race, gender, and class, and require students to take on the role or point of view of the "other" (Connell, 1995; DeKeseredy, Schwartz, & Alvi, 2000; Messerschmidt, 2000). Further, workshops could be given in local schools or community centers designed specifically to train people what to do when confronted with male-to-female abuse in public and private places. Participants should also be taught how to support victims to seek help in appropriate ways, and to work to help abusive men become peaceful (DeKeseredy et al., 2004; Hazler, 1996).

Gendered second generation CPTED policies and the other initiatives aimed at curbing woman abuse proposed in this chapter are not the only effective solutions. In fact, many more progressive strategies could easily be suggested.[12] However, all policy recommendations must be highly sensitive to the ways in which broader social forces contribute to woman abuse. As Websdale (1998) discovered in his study of woman battering in rural Kentucky, "Any social policy initiatives must use the structure of rural patriarchy, in all its intricate manifestations, as an essential frame of reference" (p. 194). Thus, sexism in all aspects of rural women's lives must be reduced and even eliminated, and the promotion of gender equality on farms, in workplaces, in families, in schools, in athletics, and so on should not be an afterthought. Ample evidence supports the claim that the "institutionalization of feminist interests" remains the keystone to specific action for building up forms of collective efficacy that reduce woman abuse in rural communities (Mazur & McBride-Stetson, 1995, p. 278).

Although second generation CPTED was discussed within the context of the issue of violence against women in rural communities, it and similar tools, like community readiness, can be used across a broad spectrum of crime issues. They are tools for activists, that is, for practitioners who advocate for the health and safety of rural peoples and rural communities.

It may seem ironic given our continuous criticism of the mainstream criminological version of collective efficacy that the authors would turn around and advocate the improvement of social cohesion in rural communities to combat violence against women and to help solve other crime issues. However, all communities, even small ones, are composed of complex networks of people (Liepins, 2000; Oetting & Donnermeyer, 1998), and reducing woman abuse and other violent crimes in rural communities requires building social cohesiveness and thus tapping into these networks in order to assure that these networks are as strong as those which enable violence (DeKeseredy & Schwartz, 2009; Lee, 2008). Hence, there is a direct link between policy and practice and theory and concepts; in this case, the idea, based mostly on rural-focused research and a critical perspective, that collective efficacy both enables and constrains crime. By positing that collective efficacy is not one-dimensional, the concept is freed up to help define strategies and actions for solving problems across a whole society, as well as within its specific places.

Indigenous justice[13]

More today than ever, critical criminologists fully recognize that progressive people of all walks of life cannot eliminate one form of inequality, like patriarchy, by ignoring others. One type, in particular, that has historically plagued many rural parts of the world is the oppression of Indigenous people. Unfortunately, criminology in general has not done much to accurately describe their plight and to help their struggle for change. In fact, as Maori scholar Juan Marcellus Tauri (2013) observes, most criminological work on Indigenous issues has done more harm than good:

> Contrary to the claims of adherents such as Weatherburn (2010), the majority of criminological material that is influencing public policy and media discourse on the Indigenous question, emanates from approaches that are predominantly quantitative in method, and largely "Aboriginal free" in terms of data gathering and engagement with the research population. The body of work that is considered of value to the policy sector and mainstream media is predominantly statistically focused and government funded.... [T]his paradigm ... avoids critical analysis of the policymaking process. It avoids or sidelines complicated, messy structural determinants such as racist policing, racist court processes, racist government policy and legislation.... These supposedly difficult-to-measure determinants of Indigenous marginalization are often dismissed through flippant and empirically weak contentions that institutional bias and structural determination have dominated (and negatively impacted) Aboriginal policymaking.
>
> *(pp. 219–220)*

To be sure, there is much crime, especially violence against women and children, in Indigenous communities. For example, only about 3% of the 35 million Canadian residents identify themselves as Aboriginal, but it is estimated that they are 12.5 times more likely to be victims of robbery or of physical or sexual assault than non-Aboriginal people (Perreault, 2011; Siegel & McCormick, 2012). Most of the crimes committed by Canadian Aboriginal people, though, are "native-on-native" (Restoule, 2009); however, these harms cannot be adequately addressed without a thorough, sophisticated understanding of colonialism. It is defined here as "the systematic oppression of people through a variety of assimilationist measures that are intended to eradicate the peoples and/or their sense of individual and cultural identity" (Restoule, 2009, p. 272).

In many parts of the world, including Canada, Australia, and the U.S.A., Indigenous people are much more likely to live in overcrowded housing, suffer from major health problems, and live in poverty than members of dominant cultures (e.g., those of European descent). These factors are strong and well-known determinants of crime. Further, Aboriginal people in Australia, North America, and elsewhere have been devastated by the loss of rural job opportunities in the last few decades, a problem that also contributes to a myriad of crimes (Hogg & Carrington, 2006; Hunter, 1999; Malley-Morrison & Hines, 2004).

If, as Cowlishaw (2013, p. 245) reminds us, that "crime is an everyday matter" in Indigenous communities, the same can be said about "over-policing" and other racist criminal justice practices (Perry, 2009). Consider the problems that routinely plague Canadian Aboriginal people described in Box 4.4 by Restoule (2009, p. 259). These issues have contributed to the recent emergence of "Idle No More," which is a nation-wide, grass-roots, Indigenous protest movement that is also heavily fueled by recent Canadian federal legislation that threatens Aboriginal sovereignty and resources.[14]

Box 4.4 Aboriginal people and the criminal justice system

- Aboriginal people spend more time in pretrial detention.
- Aboriginal people accused of a crime are more likely to be charged with multiple offenses and often for crimes against the system.
- Aboriginal people are more likely not to have legal representation at court proceedings.
- Aboriginal clients, especially in northern communities, where the court party flies in the day of the hearing, spend less time with their lawyers.
- Because court schedules in remote areas are poorly planned, judges may have limited time in the community.
- Aboriginal offenders are more than twice as likely to be incarcerated than non-Aboriginal offenders.

- Aboriginal Elders, who are spiritual leaders, are not given the same status as prison priests or chaplains, in all institutions.
- Aboriginal people often plead guilty because they are intimidated by the court and simply want the proceedings over with.
- Aboriginal people often commit offenses related to violence (usually against another Aboriginal person and/or a family member), social disorder, crimes against the system, or petty crimes.
- At least half of all offenses are alcohol-related.

The solutions to the problems listed in Box 4.4 require much more than cultural awareness training for criminal justice officials and community policing. The former hides the racist practices and inequality it claims to address, while the latter is based on a White or Western legal order (Perry, 2009). For Indigenous people and the small group of critical criminologists who are firmly on their side, crime in Indigenous communities and racist means of social control can only be solved with sovereignty. Unfortunately, criminal justice systems are unlikely to shed their colonial baggage soon and hence many readers of this book are unlikely to ever live to see the following model informed by Indigenous values, beliefs, and politics:

> The European adversarial approach would be replaced with one based in the principles of peacemaking, community control, and the autonomy of individuals. In all likelihood, the formal charging of individuals would frequently be replaced by mediation between parties. The courts might be radically different than those seen in White communities. They would be less adversarial and would stress conflict resolution and peacemaking. A wide variety of "sentencing" options would be available, and offenders would only be jailed if they were seen to pose a danger to the community.
>
> *(Skoog, 1996, p. 128)*

Even if the above "alterNatives" to traditional criminal justice were fully implemented, crime can only be reduced in Indigenous communities if the following are done to enhance Aboriginal people's quality of life with the assistance of the private and public sector:

- improving employment opportunities;
- providing better housing;
- improving health care;
- creating better future prospects for youth; and
- offering an education informed by traditional Aboriginal pedagogy.

(Tomaszewski, 1997, p. 116)

These steps should be taken right away in countries such as Canada because, as demonstrated by the "Idle No More" movement, the anger of many young Indigenous people is intensifying each day. As *Toronto Star* reporter Tim Harper (2013) observes, unless the Canadian federal government sincerely responds to Indigenous people's concerns, "Flash mobs could turn to violence; rail border and highway blockades will not be as brief nor as polite."

Crimes of the powerful[15]

The hurtful ways in which Indigenous people are treated by various levels of mainstream government around the world are defined by critical criminologists as state crimes, which fall under the broader category of "crimes of the powerful."[16] Critical criminologists have played a vital role in directing attention to serious harms caused by government agencies and private businesses,[17] and a growing number of them are focusing on crimes committed by these formal organizations in rural areas. For example, unlike most other criminological anthologies, the *Routledge International Handbook of Green Criminology*, edited by critical criminologists Nigel South and Avi Brisman (2013), includes a sizeable portion of material on environmental crimes that occur in rural areas around the world. This is a major step forward for criminology and hopefully more scholars will follow in the contributors' ground-breaking footsteps.

To have a truly just society, one that is sincerely and explicitly committed to protecting its citizens, "crimes in the suites," in the words of Reiman and Leighton (2010), must be "prosecuted and punished as vigorously as crime in the streets" (p. 206). This only makes sense, given that a large literature, such as the body of work recently reviewed by Friedrichs and Rothe (2012) shows that corporate crime is far more economically, socially, and environmentally injurious than muggings, theft, and other variants of street crime. Yet, there is no reason to believe that government officials in a capitalist society are going to launch a "war on corporate crime" in the near future. And, how often do we hear cries for "three strikes and you're out" in relation to corporate crime? In fact, some evidence suggests that governments around the world, especially in North America, are making it easier for corporations to threaten our well-being. A prime example is recent Canadian federal government's pared-down environmental protection laws (Whittington, 2013), which helped trigger the "Idle No More" movement.

Nevertheless, many people are using social media to publicly shame corporations and to sensitize thousands of people to the damage done by corporations in rural and other areas (DeKeseredy, 2011a). Their actions at a national and even international level are similar in philosophy to actions at the local level as defined by second generation CPTED. Furthermore, in response to green crimes, a growing number of people around the world are engaging in what Rob White (2011) refers to as "transnational activism." In some cases this involves:

- campaigns and actions that disrupt corporate operations;
- corporate vilification campaigns relating to their "clean" and "green" image;
- campaigns against overseas customers of corporate products; and
- corporate campaigns targeting shareholders, investors, and banks.

(p. 144)

Albeit rapidly disappearing, there are factories in some rural communities and like their urban counterparts, many rural folks who work in such environments are at great risk of experiencing corporate violence (DeKeseredy, Ellis, & Alvi, 2005). Following DeKeseredy & Hinch (1991, p. 100), this crime is defined here as:

> any behavior undertaken in the name of a corporation by decision makers, or other persons in authority within the corporation, that

endangers the health and safety of employees or other persons who are affected by that behavior. Even acts of omission, in which decision makers, etc., refuse to take action to reduce or eliminate known health and safety risks, must be considered corporate violence. It is the impact the action has on the victim, not the intent of the act, which determines, whether or not it is violence.

The critical criminological "knee-jerk reaction" to corporate violence against workers is, not surprisingly, the same as what Reiman and Leighton (2010) call for: stricter prosecution and punishment. There is, of course, much corporate resistance to this solution and it is not likely to happen in this current neo-liberal era. Thus, another strategy suggested by some critical criminologists (e.g., DeKeseredy et al., 2005) is to promote the practice of workplace democracy. One of the prime measures would be to add workers and community members to corporations' boards of directors (Messerschmidt, 1986). Presumably, workers could help democratize the workplace and improve the health and well-being of laborers who are at great risk of either being killed or injured in the workplace. Further, community members could ensure that corporate decisions address broader social issues, such as environmental hazards, plant locations, exploitation of natural resources, prices, and product safety.

If workplaces are democratized, there is a good chance that management and labor will develop union-dominated committees on health and safety, such as those found in Sweden (DeKeseredy et al., 2005; Messserschmidt, 1986). Some examples of the tasks performed by these committees are: (1) vetoing dangerous machinery, work processes, and construction; (2) selecting and directing the work of medical personnel, safety engineers, and industrial hygienists; (3) interviewing candidates for health and safety jobs; (4) making sure that proposed budgets include funds for health and safety; and (5) shutting down hazardous projects until they have been rectified (DeKeseredy & Goff, 1992; Engler, 1986; Messerschmidt, 1986).

We propose this solution with much pessimism because of "right to work" legislation that is popping up like weeds across the United States (see Box 2.1) and is strongly supported by Tim Hudak, leader of the Progressive Conservative Party of Ontario, Canada, at the time of writing this chapter. They are not the current governing party in Ontario, but the "Tories," as they are called in Ontario, stand a very good chance of winning the next election, and aggressively targeting unions and public sector workers will be the first item on their political agenda. Unions are certainly shrinking in size in North America and it seems that workplace democracy will be difficult, if not impossible, to achieve if corporate greed and government support for "union bashing" continues to flourish.

Summary

To the best of our knowledge, this is the first scholarly book chapter to outline a critical criminological blueprint for curbing crime and improving social control in rural communities. Many progressive readers, albeit supportive of our recommendations, are likely to contend that we have overlooked or ignored other important policy proposals. This is not necessarily a bad thing because it provides our colleagues opportunities to supplement what we have covered here. As rural critical criminologists, we are eager to see the development of more policies and the publication of more critical articles, book chapters, and books on crime and justice in rural communities. There is plenty more work to do and it is time to think more critically about rural crime.

It is not surprising that the bulk of the policies discussed in this chapter are out of place in a traditional or mainstream criminology book. For example, many criminologists would argue that job creation is a topic that belongs in urban policy, political sociology, or public administration. The problem is that real life does not play itself out along the bureaucratic lines set up by universities and government agencies. It is well known in criminology that your level of income can affect how you behave, and the fact that the labor department is located in a separate building from the criminal justice department does not affect that truth. In real life, jobs, childcare, nutrition, welfare, and many other events affect your life. It is mainly in textbooks that they are segregated (DeKeseredy & Schwartz, 1996).

Also scattered throughout this chapter is much pessimism and doubt because there is overwhelming right-wing resistance in many parts of the world to everything we suggested. Left-wing criminological thinking in universities and colleges, so-called bastions of liberal thought, is also under siege (DeKeseredy, 2012). Unfortunately, progressives have much to be depressed about. Nevertheless, the struggle for social justice, democracy, and peaceful societies must continue and we can derive much strength and faith in social change from the Canadian Indigenous "Idle No More" movement and the international "Occupy" movement.[18] Perhaps, then, it is most fitting to end this chapter by quoting U.S. critical criminologist Elliott Currie (2013):

> A revived, committed and unapologetic movement based on small-letter social democratic principles does have the potential to inspire, and to mobilize broad constituencies behind real solutions to the endemic problems of predatory capitalism. This is not to say that it can simply redeploy the tools it has relied on in the past. An effective movement will need to push the traditional social democratic envelope, to tackle problems that have stymied it.

> *(p. 14)*

NOTES

1 Rural crime: myths and realities

1 This section includes revised versions of work published previously by DeKeseredy (2007b, 2009) and DeKeseredy and Dragiewicz (2012a).

2 See DeKeseredy (2011a) and DeKeseredy and Dragiewicz (2012b) for in-depth reviews of contemporary critical criminological schools of thought.

3 Author of the best-selling 1985 book *Thinking About Crime*, James Q. Wilson, who passed away in 2012, is a prime example of criminologist who held this belief.

4 This section includes modified parts of work published previously by DeKeseredy and Schwartz (2009) and DeKeseredy et al. (2007).

5 Similar to Durkheim's (1964) view of rural life as "mechanical solidarity," Tönnies's (1955) work on urbanism spawned the concept of *Gemeinschaft*, a term now widely used in sociology. Briefly, Tönnies argued that, on the one hand, in traditional rural, or *Gemeinschaft* societies, people have strong attachments to each other. He conceptualizes modern, urban, *Gesellschaft* societies, on the other hand, as the "antithesis" of *Gemeinschaft* because they are tenuous, impersonal, and heterogeneous (Donnermeyer et al., 2006).

6 This section includes revised parts of work published earlier by DeKeseredy et al. (2007) and Donnermeyer (2012).

7 See Donnermeyer et al. (2006) and Weisheit et al. (2006) for reviews of this literature.

8 See DeKeseredy et al. (2007) and Donnermeyer (2012) for reviews of these studies.

9 See DeKeseredy and Schwartz (2013) for an in-depth review of the theoretical, empirical, and policy literature on male peer support and woman abuse.

10 Despite studies that challenge the logic of mainstream collective efficacy theory (e.g., DeKeseredy & Schwartz, 2009; Venkatesh, 1997), Robert Sampson (2012), one of the pioneers of this ecological perspective, asserts that "The logic of collective efficacy theory is not disproven by the intermingling of criminal and noncriminal networks" (p. 153).

11 This section includes modified parts of work published previously by DeKeseredy et al. (2013), DeKeseredy and Schwartz (2009), and Donnermeyer (2012).

12 For the purpose of this study, Rennison et al. (in press) operationalized violence by combining measures of attempted and completed rape/sexual assault, robbery, aggravated assault, and simple assault.

13 See Mooney (2012) for a brief history of the Centre for Contemporary Cultural Studies.

14 See Donnermeyer (2012) for these recent materials on rural crime and social control, as well as Chapter 3 in this book.

15 This is the subtitle of DeKeseredy et al.'s (2012) article. Parts of this section are also adapted from this article and from DeKeseredy and Schwartz's (2009) book.

16 Like the concept "rural," the term "Appalachia" is defined in many ways. However, it generally refers to a geographic region associated with the Appalachian Mountains and the people who live there (DeKeseredy & Schwartz, 2009).

17 Modleski (1986) and Sconce (1995) are examples of scholars who share this interpretation.

18 See Brownridge (2009), DeKeseredy and Schwartz (2009), and Basile and Black (2011) for reviews of the extant North American literature on lethal and non-lethal male-to-female separation/divorce assaults.

19 See DeKeseredy et al. (2012) for a more in-depth sociological analysis of these three men's motives for putting sharks in the lake.

20 See DeKeseredy and Schwartz (2013) for a review of these studies.

21 As well, individualistic perspectives on crime, such as biosocial theories, are becoming more popular in certain academic groups (DeKeseredy, 2012).

22 Radical feminists see male power and privilege as the "root cause of all social relations," inequality, and other social problems. For radical feminists, the most important set of social relations in any society is found in patriarchy. All other social relations, such as class, are secondary and originate from male–female relations (Beirne & Messerschmidt, 2011, quote from p. 208; Daly & Chesney-Lind, 1988; Renzetti, 2012).

2 Thinking critically about rural crime

1 C. Wright Mills (1916–1962) was a radical sociologist for his time and he was sharply critical of research divorced from theory. His 1959 book *The Sociological Imagination* continues to be widely read and cited around the world. Included in this volume is this famous statement: "Be a good craftsman: Avoid any rigid set of procedures. Avoid the fetishism of method and technique" (p. 224).

2 In response to sharp criticisms of instrumental Marxist perspectives on the state in the late 1970s, several theorists developed an alternative Marxist explanation of the state and law – structural Marxism. Guided by the writings of Louis Althusser (1971), Nicos Poulantzas (1973), and Isaac Balbus

(1977), criminologists such as Quinney argued that the state is not simply a tool or instrument of capitalists. Although they acknowledged some link between the state and the interests of business elites, they viewed the state as "relatively autonomous" from individual capitalists. In other words, to protect the long-term interests of capitalism, the state must occasionally act against the short-term interests of particular members of the ruling class (Gold, Lo, & Wright, 1975).

3 See Chambliss and Zatz (1993) for an excellent collection of articles on structural contradictions theory.

4 For example, see Chambliss (1975), Gordon (1971), Greenberg (1981), and Spitzer (1975).

5 This section includes revised portions of work published previously by Donnermeyer and DeKeseredy (2008).

6 Ellis' (1987) critique of Taylor et al.'s (1973) book is relevant here:

> *The New Criminology* promises a "full blown Marxist" and a "fully social theory" of crime and deviance. It delivers neither. A rather general statement of things to be taken into account in formulating an explanation of crime and deviance is not a theory, much less a full blown, fully social Marxist one. On the other hand, their critical analyses of existing Marxist theories is very good.
>
> *(p. 67)*

7 Edited by pioneering British feminist criminologist Pat Carlen, *Criminal Justice Matters,* 70 (Winter 2007/2008) is an outstanding collection of short articles on politics, economy, and crime.

8 See Potter (2007) for a collection of essays on the racial implications of Hurricane Katrina.

9 For example, after nearly 70 years of operation, in 2002, the Rocky Shoes and Boots factory closed in Nelsonville, Ohio, and moved to Puerto Rico. None of its 67 displaced workers were offered replacement jobs (Price, 2002).

10 See DeKeseredy and Schwartz (1996) for an in-depth review of the Marxist debates about the state and law that occurred during that time period.

11 Left realism emerged in the mid-1980s in the United Kingdom and in the United States. The roots of left realism are found in the writings of Jock Young (1975, 1979), Tony Platt (1978), and Ian Taylor (1981), but this school of thought was not expressed formally until the publication of John Lea and Jock Young's (1984) *What Is to Be Done about Law and Order?* Shortly after this seminal work came Elliott Currie's (1985) *Confronting Crime: An American Challenge,* which arguably, marked the official birth of North American left realism. See DeKeseredy and Schwartz (2012) for an in-depth review of left realists' theoretical, empirical, and policy contributions.

12 This section includes modified parts of work published previously by DeKeseredy et al. (2004) and DeKeseredy and Schwartz (2009, 2013). 888

13 See DeKeseredy and Schwartz (2013) for a history of male peer support theory and for in-depth reviews of the empirical and theoretical contributions

DeKeseredy and Schwartz have made over the years to a sociological under-standing of male peer support and woman abuse in a variety of contexts.

14 Many feminist scholars, advocates, and activists correctly point out that the first question blames females for the abuse they experience in intimate rela-tionships. As well, as Stark (2007, p. 130) notes: "It is the men who stay, not their partners." Indeed, "there is no greater challenge in the abuse field than getting men to exit from abusive relationships" (as noted frequently by others too, e.g., Bancroft, 2002; DeKeseredy & Schwartz, 2009).

15 This section includes revised portions of work published previously by DeKeseredy et al. (2007) and DeKeseredy and Schwartz (2013).

16 Go to http://cjrc.osu.edu/ for more information on the CJRC.

17 Joe agrees.

3 Creating the critical in rural criminology

1 This article was published in the only issue of the *International Journal of Rural Crime*. A second attempt at the development of a rural criminology journal is now underway, and looks more likely to sustain itself. It is the *International Journal of Rural Criminology* at the following web address: https://kb.osu.edu/dspace/handle/1811/51123/browse?type=title, or it can be found via a search on Google. The original articles from the *International Journal of Rural Crime* can also be found at this site.

2 If Sampson (2012) can call forms of social organization which facilitate crime "anti-collective efficacy," we can call the flawed logic of con-temporary and latter-day expressions of social disorganization theory as described in Chapter 1, Myth #2 (collective efficacy = low crime, and social disorganization = high crime) the "antithesis."

3 Here is what Merton wrote in *Social Theory and Social Structure* (1949, p. 40):

> In its more empirically oriented and analytically precise forms, func-tional analysis is often regarded with suspicion by those who consider an existing social structure as externally fixed and beyond change. The more exacting form of functional analysis includes, not only a study of the functions of existing social structures, but also a study of their dys-functions for diversely situated individuals, subgroups or social strata, and the more inclusive society.

Building on this observation in his 1972 *American Journal of Sociology* article on the functions of poverty, Gans wrote (p. 276):

> In discussing the functions of poverty, I shall identify functions for groups and aggregates; specifically, interest groups, socioeconomic classes, and other population aggregates, for example, those with shared values or similar statuses. This definitional approach is based on the assumption that almost every social system – and of course every society – is composed of groups or aggregates with different interests and values, so that, as Merton put it (1949, p. 51) "items may be functional for

some individuals and subgroups and dysfunctional for others." Indeed, frequently one group's functions are another group's dysfunctions.

Yet, like an addict who may never recover from one's dependency on the powerful effects of a drug, so many in the mainstream of criminology fall back on notions of *Gemeinschaft*, cohesion, solidarity, social capital, and collective efficacy as if their functionality is universal for all within a place, whether that place is large or small, even though they would nod their heads affirmatively to the admonishments of Merton and Gans.

4 Several of the articles in this citation list utilize something other than social disorganization theory, but closely allied with its manner of considering causality at the community level and crime, and a few attempt a fusion of social disorganization theory with other theories from mainstream criminology. Most notably, see Spano and Nagy (2005) who use concepts from routine activities theory and the concept of social guardianship; Lee and associates (Lee, 2008; Lee & Bartkowski, 2004b; Lee et al., 2003) for the application of civic community theory and concepts related to social capital; Donnermeyer, Barclay, and Jobes' (in press) attempt to compare social disorganization and conflict theory; and Wells and Weisheit (2012) who conduct a comparative statistical analysis of social disorganization and civic communities theories.

5 Although mainstream criminology blissfully ignores the simultaneity of social organization for enabling and constraining crime, writers of novels and television soap operas – from Mark Twain's short story "The Man Who Corrupted Hadleyburg" to *Days of Our Lives*, the long running American soap opera set in the fictional town of Salem – know it and use it to construct convoluted plots and surprise endings. Inevitably, the stalwarts of these fictionalized localities have hidden agendas and secret sins which would ruin their reputations and reduce their influence over others if exposed. They use their power to impose a social order and morality upon others according to their self-interests. Those more marginalized and stigmatized within these pretend places express a variety of oppositional and/or retreatist behaviors and desperately seek to discover the faults of the powerful for their own vested interests, or blindly try to conform, hence feeling as if they have joined the ranks of the elite. Alliances form and collapse, and re-form again. Perhaps the mainstream journals would better advance scholarship in criminology by publishing a soap opera digest or reprinting the works of Twain, Shakespeare, and other literary giants who knew long ago what the urban-centric proponents of social disorganization theory and its latter-day expressions have apparently never figured out.

6 Lyrics from the Waylon Jennings song that is the opening music for the U.S. television show, *Dukes of Hazzard*.

7 This section features revised sections of material published previously by DeKeseredy and Donnermeyer (2012), Donnermeyer (2012), and Donnermeyer et al. (2011).

4 Looking forward and glancing back: research, policy, and practice

1 One of the authors was a reviewer several years back for a manuscript sub-mitted to one of the top criminology journals in the U.S.A. The sample included subjects from Milwaukee, a metropolitan area of over one million persons. When this reviewer received the comments of other reviewers, sent out courtesy of the editor, he was bemused by the statement of one reviewer who found the study insignificant because it was not from a "big city like Los Angeles," suggesting that Milwaukee was too small as a research site for important criminology scholarship. Imagine what this reviewer would have said in response to a study from a rural location!

2 *The International Journal of Rural Criminology* is published through the "Know-ledge Bank" of The Ohio State University libraries. It is an online journal, published twice each year.

3 As South Korea's government clearly demonstrates, strengthening a country's cultural and entertainment sector yields major economic gains (Klassen, 2013).

4 U.S. sociologist Harold Garfinkle (1956) coined the term "degradation ceremony." He states, "Any communicative work between persons, whereby the public identity of an actor is transformed into something looked on as lower in the local scheme of social types, will be called a 'status degradation ceremony'" (p. 420).

5 This term was frequently mentioned by the press, policy-makers, academics, and the general public at the end of 2012 and in early 2013. It is used to describe major U.S. federal tax increases and spending cuts that were due to occur at the end of 2012 and in early 2013 (Masters, 2012).

6 This section includes modified parts of work published previously by DeKe-seredy and Schwartz (2009).

7 Queen's University is in Kingston, Ontario, Canada.

8 This section includes revised portions of work published previously by DeKeseredy et al. (2004, 2009) and DeKeseredy and Schwartz (2009).

9 See Websdale and Johnson (2005) for more information on these programs.

10 See DeKeseredy and Schwartz (2013), DeKeseredy et al. (2000), Funk (1993, 2006), Katz (2006), Kimmel and Mosmiller (1992), and Thorne-Finch (1992) for more in-depth information on the pro-feminist men's movement.

11 See Alvi, Schwartz, DeKeseredy, and Maume (2001) and Renzetti and Maier (2002) for data on women's fear of crime in North American public housing.

12 See DeKeseredy and Schwartz (2009) and Websdale (1998) for more detailed answers to the question "What is to be done about woman abuse in rural communities?"

13 This is the title of a section in a critical criminological anthology edited by Carrington, Ball, O'Brien, and Tauri (2013).

14 Go to http://idlenomore.ca/ for more information on the "Idle No More" movement.

15 This is the title of Frank Pearce's (1976) path-breaking Marxist analysis of corporate and organized crime. As well, this section includes modified sections of work published earlier by DeKeseredy et al. (2005).

16 Defining state crime is subject to much debate. See Barak (2011) for an in-depth review of the key definitional debates.

17 See Friedrichs and Rothe (2012) for an in-depth review of the critical criminological literature on crimes of the powerful.

18 The "Occupy" movement first started as the "Occupy Wall Street" movement on September 17, 2011, in New York City's Zuccotti Park. "Occupy" is a grass-roots struggle against corporate greed and social and economic inequality. Go to www.occupytogether.org/aboutoccupy/ for more information on "Occupy."

REFERENCES

Adams, D., & Goldbard, A. (2001). *Creative community: The art of cultural development*. New York: Rockefeller Foundation.

Althusser, L. (1971). *Lenin and philosophy and other essays*. New York: Left Books.

Alvi, S., Schwartz, M.D., DeKeseredy, W.S., & Maume, M.O. (2001). Women's fear of crime in Canadian public housing. *Violence Against Women, 7*, 638–661.

Anderson, D.M. (1999). Sexual abuse, professional boundaries, and the rural world. *Journal of Child Sexual Abuse, 8*, 85–93.

Arthur, J.A. (1991). Socioeconomic predictors of crime in rural Georgia. *Criminal Justice Review, 16*, 29–41.

Atkins, N. (2013). U.S. school killer Adam Lanza wore earplugs to drown screams of victims. *Mirror Online*. Retrieved January 8, 2013, from www. mirror.co.uk/news/world-news/sandy-hook-adam-lanza-wore-1524092.

Baker, R.B. (2008, November). The effects of rural disorganization on crime: Investigating official crime data. Paper presented at the annual meeting of the American Society of Criminology. St. Louis, Missouri.

Balbus, I. (1977). Commodity form and legal form: An essay on the "relative autonomy" of the law. *Law and Society Review, 11*, 571–588.

Bancroft, L. (2002). *Why does he do that? Inside the minds of angry and controlling men*. New York: Penguin.

Bankston, W.B., & Allen, H.D. (1980). Rural social areas and patterns of homicide: An analysis of lethal violence in Louisiana. *Rural Sociology, 45*, 223–237.

Barak, G. (2011). Revisiting crimes by the capitalist state. In D.L. Rothe & C.W. Mullins (Eds.), *State crime: Current perspectives* (pp. 35–48). New Brunswick, NJ: Rutgers University Press.

Barclay, E. (2003). *Crime with rural communities: The dark side of "Gemeinschaft"* (Ph.D. dissertation). Armidale, New South Wales, The University of New England.

Barclay, E., & Donnermeyer, J.F. (2007). Community and crime in rural Australia. In E. Barclay, J.F. Donnermeyer, J. Scott, & R. Hogg (Eds.), *Crime in rural Australia* (pp. 44–54). Annandale, NSW, Australia: Federation Press.

Barclay, E., & Donnermeyer, J.F. (2011). Crime and security on agricultural operations. *Security Journal, 24*, 1–18.

Barclay, E., Donnermeyer, J.F., & Jobes, P.C. (2004). The dark side of Gemeinschaft. *Crime Prevention and Community Safety, 6*, 7–22.

Barclay, E., Scott, J., & Donnermeyer, J.F. (2011). Policing the outback: Impacts of isolation and integration in an Australian context. In R.I. Mawby & R. Yarwood (Eds.), *Rural policing and policing the rural: A constable countryside?* (pp. 33–44). Farnham, UK: Ashgate.

Barclay, E., Donnermeyer, J.F., Scott, J., & Hogg, R. (Eds.). (2007). *Crime in rural Australia*. Annandale, NSW, Australia: Federation Press.

Barnett, C., & Mencken, F.C. (2002). Social disorganization theory and the contextual nature of crime in non-metropolitan counties. *Rural Sociology, 67*, 372–393.

Barron, M., & Kimmel, M. (2000). Sexual violence in three pornographic media: Toward a sociological explanation. *Journal of Sex Research, 8*, 161–168.

Barton, A., Storey, D., & Palmer, C. (2011). A trip in the country? Policing drug use in rural settings. In R.I. Mawby & R. Yarwood (Eds.), *Rural policing and policing the rural: A constable countryside?* (pp. 147–158). Farnham, UK: Ashgate.

Basile, K.C., & Black, MC. (2011). Intimate partner violence against women. In C.M. Renzetti, J.L. Edleson, & R.K. Bergen (Eds.), *Sourcebook on violence against women* (2nd ed., pp. 111–130). Thousand Oaks, CA: Sage.

Basran, G.S., Gill, C., & MacLean, B.D. (1995). *Farmworkers and their children*. Vancouver: Collective Press.

Becker, H.S. (1973). *Outsiders: Studies in the sociology of deviance* (2nd edn.). New York: Free Press.

Beckett, K., & Sasson, T. (2000). *The politics of injustice: Crime and punishment in America*. Thousand Oaks, CA: Sage.

Beirne, P., & Messerschmidt, J.W. (2011). *Criminology: A sociological approach* (5th ed.). New York: Oxford University Press.

Bell, D. (1997). Anti-idyll: Rural horror. In P. Cloke & J. Little (Eds.), *Contested countryside cultures: Otherness, marginalization and rurality* (pp. 94–108). London: Routledge.

Bell, D. (2006). Varations on the rural idyll. In P. Cloke, T. Marsden, & P.H. Mooney (Eds.), *Handbook of Rural Studies* (pp. 149–161). London: Sage.

Bernstein, B. (2000). *Pedagogy, symbolic control and identity: Theory, research, critique*. Oxford: Rowman & Littlefield.

Berthelot, E.R., Blanchard, T.C., & Brown, T.C. (2008). Scots-Irish women and the southern culture of violence: The influence of Scots-Irish females on high rates of southern violence. *Southern Rural Sociology, 23,* 157–170.

Betowski, B. (2007). 1 in 3 boys heavy porn users, study shows. Retrieved February 23, 2007, from www.eurekalert.org/pub_releases/2007–02/uoa-oit022307.php.

Bhattacharyya, M., Bedi, A.S., & Chhachhi, A. (2011). Marital violence and women's employment and property status: Evidence from north Indian villages. *World Development, 39,* 1676–1689.

Bierstedt, R. (1957). *The social order.* New York: McGraw-Hill.

Block, C.R., & DeKeseredy, W.S. (2007). Forced sex and leaving intimate relationships: Results of the Chicago women's health risk study. *Women's Health and Urban Life, 6,* 6–24.

Bohm, R.M., & Walker, J.T. (Eds.). (2013). *Demystifying crime and criminal justice* (2nd ed.). New York: Oxford University Press.

Bouffard, L.A., & Muftić, L.R. (2006). The "rural mystique": Social disorganization and violence beyond urban communities. *Western Criminology Review, 7,* 56–66.

Bourgois, P. (1995). *In search of respect: Selling crack in El Barrio.* New York: Cambridge University Press.

Boyle, T. (2007, June 29). Small towns have higher crime rates. *Toronto Star,* p. A1.

Brandwein, R.A. (1999). Family violence, women, and welfare. In R.A. Brandwein (Ed.), *Battered women, children, and welfare reform: The ties that bind* (pp. 3–16). Thousand Oaks, CA: Sage.

Brassard, A. (2003). Integrating the planning process and second-generation CPTED. *The CPTED Journal, 2,* 46–53.

Brennan, J., & Stanford, J. (2012, December 28). Inequality's exorbitant price. *Toronto Star,* p. A19.

Brennan, R.J. (2012, May 23). Economic equality for women still centuries off: Parity won't occur until year 2593, study shows. *Toronto Star,* p. A3.

Bridges, A.J., & Anton, C. (in press). Pornography and violence against women. In J. Sigel & R. Denmark (Eds.), *Violence against women across the lifespan: An international perspective.* New York: Praeger.

Bridges, A.J., & Jensen, R. (2011). Pornography. In C.M. Renzetti, J.L. Edleson, & R. Kennedy Bergen (Eds.), *Sourcebook on violence against women* (2nd ed., pp. 133–148). Thousand Oaks, CA: Sage.

Bridges, A.J., Wosnitzer, R., Scharrer, E., Sun, C., & Liberman, R. (2010). Aggression and sexual behavior in best-selling pornography videos: A content analysis. *Violence Against Women, 16,* 1065–1085.

Brosi, M., Foubert, J.D., Bannon, R.S., & Yandell, G. (2011). Effects of sorority members' pornography use on bystander intervention in sexual assault situation and rape myth acceptance. *Oracle, 6*, 26–35.

Brown, D.L., & Schafft, K.A. (2011). *Rural people and communities in the twenty-first century: Resilience and transformation.* Boston: Polity Press.

Brown, D.L., & Swanson, L.E. (Eds.). (2003). *Challenges for rural America in the 21st century.* University Park: Pennsylvania State University Press.

Brownridge, D.A. (2009). *Violence against women: Vulnerable populations.* New York: Routledge.

Bull, M. (2007). Alcohol and drug problems in rural and regional Australia. In J. Scott, R. Hogg, E. Barclay, & J. Donnermeyer (Eds.), *Crime in Rural Australia* (pp. 72–85). Annandale, NSW, Australia: Federation Press.

Burd-Sharps, S., Lewis, K., & Borges Martins, E. (2009). *The measure of America: American human development report 2008–2009.* New York: Columbia University Press.

Bursik, R.J., Jr. (1988). Social disorganization and theories of crime and delinquency: Problems and prospects. *Criminology, 26*, 519–551.

Bursik, R.J., Jr. (1999). The informal control of crime through neighborhood networks. *Sociological Focus, 32*, 85–97.

Buttel, F.H., & Goodman, D. (1989). Class, state, technology and international food regimes. *Sociologia Ruralis, 29*, 86–92.

Campbell, H. (2000). The glass phallus: Pub(lic) masculinity and drinking in rural New Zealand. *Rural Sociology, 65*, 532–536.

Campbell, H. (2006). Real men, real locals, and real workers: Realizing masculinity in small-town New Zealand. In H. Campbell, M. Mayerfeld Bell, & M. Finney (Eds.), *Country boys: Masculinity and rural life* (pp. 87–104). University Park, PA: Pennsylvania State University Press.

Cancian, M., & Danziger, S. (2009). Changing poverty and changing antipoverty policies. *Focus, 26*, 1–5.

Cancino, J.M. (2005). The utility of social capital and collective efficacy: Social control policy in non-metropolitan settings. *Criminal Justice Policy Review, 16*, 287–318.

Carbone-Lopez, K., Gatewood Owens, J., & Miller, J. (2012). Women's "storylines" of methamphetamine initiation in the Midwest. *Journal of Drug Issues, 42*, 226–246.

Caringella, S. (2009). *Addressing rape reform in law and practice.* New York: Columbia University Press.

Carrington, K. (2007). Crime in rural and regional areas. In E. Barclay, J.F. Donnermeyer, J. Scott, & R. Hogg (Eds.), *Crime in rural Australia* (pp. 27–43). Annandale, NSW, Australia: Federation Press.

Carrington, K., & Scott, J. (2008). Masculinity, rurality and violence. *British Journal of Criminology, 48*, 641–666.

Carrington, K., Hogg, R., & McIntosh, A. (2011). The resource boom's underbelly: The criminological impact of mining development. *Australian and New Zealand Journal of Criminology, 44*, 335–354.

Carrington, K., McIntosh, A., & Scott, J. (2010). Globalization, frontier masculinities and violence: Booze, blokes and brawls. *British Journal of Criminology, 50*, 393–413.

Carrington, K., Ball, M., O'Brien, E. & Tauri, J. (Eds.). (2013). *Crime, justice and social democracy*. New York: Palgrave Macmillan.

Carrington, K., McIntosh, A., Hogg, R., & Scott, J. (2013). Rural masculinities and the internationalisation of violence in agricultural communities. *International Journal of Rural Criminology, 2*, 1–23.

Carter, T.J., Phillips, H.G., Donnermeyer, J.F., & Wurschmidt, T.N. (Eds.). (1982). *Rural crime: Integrating research and prevention*. Totowa, NJ: Allanheld, Osmun.

Catalyst. (2012, August 13). Women's earnings and income. Retrieved January 11, 2013, from www.catalyst.org/knowledge/women's-earnings-and-income.

CBC News. (2012, February 9). Big-city crime? Murder rates are higher in rural Canada. Retrieved December 5, 2012, from www.cbc.ca/news/canada/toronto/story/2012/02/09/f-crime-rates-urban–rural.html.

Ceccato, V., & Dolmen, L. (2011). Crime in rural Sweden. *Applied Geography, 31*, 119–135.

Chakraborti, N., & Garland, J. (Eds.). (2004). *Rural racism*. Portland, OR: Willan.

Chambliss, W.J. (1964). A sociological analysis of the law of vagrancy. *Social Problems, 12*, 46–67.

Chambliss, W.J. (1973). Elites and the creation of criminal law. In W. Chambliss (Ed.), *Sociological readings in the conflict perspective* (pp. 430–444). Reading, MA: Addison-Wesley.

Chambliss, W.J. (1975). Toward a political economy of crime. *Theory and Society, 2*, Summer, 149–170.

Chambliss, W.J. (1986). On lawmaking. In S. Brickey & E. Comack (Eds.), *The social basis of law: Critical readings in the sociology of law* (pp. 27–51). Toronto: Garamond.

Chambliss, W.J. (1993). The creation of criminal law and crime control in Britain and America. In W.J. Chambliss & M.S. Zatz (Eds.), *Making law: The state, the law, and structural contradictions* (pp. 3–35). Bloomington: Indiana University Press.

Chambliss, W.J., & Zatz, M.S. (Eds.). (1993). *Making law: The state, the law, and structural contradictions*. Bloomington: Indiana University Press.

Chapman, A. (2009). Illiterate hillbillies or vintage individuals: Perceptions of the Appalachian dialect. *Commonplace*. Retrieved September 24, 2012, from www.mhlearningsolutions.com/commonplace/index.php?q=node/5514.

Chavez, E.L., Edwards, R., & Oetting, E.R. (1989). Mexican-American and white America dropouts' drug use, health status and involvement in violence. *Public Health Reports, 104,* 594–604.

Chesney-Lind, M. (2007). Epilogue: Criminal justice, gender and diversity: A call for passion and public criminology. In S.L. Miller (Ed.), *Criminal justice research and practice: Diverse voices in the field* (pp. 210–220). Boston: Northeastern University Press.

Christenson, J.A., & Garkovich, L.E. (1985). Fifty years of rural sociology: Status, trends and impressions. *Rural Sociology, 50,* 503–522.

Chu, R., Rivera, C., & Loftin, C. (2000). Herding and homicide: An examination of the Nisbett-Reaves hypothesis. *Social Forces, 78,* 971–987.

Clark, J.P., & Wenninger, E.P. (1962). Socio-economic class and area as correlates of illegal behavior among juveniles. *American Sociological Review, 27,* 826–834.

Cleveland, G., & Saville, G. (2003). An introduction to second generation CPTED – part 1. Retrieved February 22, 2013 from www.CPTED.net.

Clifford, M. (1998). *Environmental crime: Enforcement, policy and social responsibility.* Gaithersburg, MD: Aspen.

Clinard, M. (1942). The process of urbanization and criminal behavior: A study of culture conflict. *American Journal of Sociology, 48,* 202–213.

Clinard, M. (1944). Rural criminal offenders. *American Journal of Sociology, 50,* 38–45.

Clinard, M.B., & Yeager, P.C. (1980). *Corporate crime: The first comprehensive account of illegal practices among America's top corporations.* New York: The Free Press.

Cloke, P., & Little, J. (1997). *Contested countryside cultures: Otherness, marginalisation, and rurality.* London: Routledge.

Cloke, P., & Milbourne, P. (1992). Deprivation and lifestyles in rural Wales – II. Rurality and the cultural dimension. *Journal of Rural Studies, 8,* 359–371.

Clover, C.J. (1992). *Men, women, and chainsaws: Gender in the modern horror film.* Princeton, NJ: Princeton University Press.

Coates, J., & Weingarten, P. (1990, April 2). U.S. marijuana cartels flower inside and out. *Chicago Tribune,* 1 and 6.

Cohen, A. (1955). *Delinquent boys: The culture of the gang.* New York: Free Press.

Conger, R.D. (1997). The special nature of rural America. In E.B. Robertson, Z. Sloboda, G.M. Boyd, L. Beatty, & N.J. Kozel (Eds.), *Rural substance use: State of knowledge and issues* (pp. 37–54). Rockville, MD: National Institutes of Health. NIDA Research Monograph 168.

Conlin, T., Chapman, J., & Benson, R. (2006). *After she leaves: A training and resource manual for volunteers and staff supporting woman abuse survivors and their children during the family law process.* Toronto: Ministry of the Attorney General.

Connell, R.W. (1995). *Masculinities*. Berkeley: University of California Press.

Coventry, G., & Palmer, D. (2008). Toward constituting a critical criminology for Australia. In T. Anthony & C. Cunneen (Eds.), *The critical criminology companion* (pp. 303–314). Sydney, Australia: Hawkins Press.

Cowan, G., & O'Brien, M. (1990). Gender and survival vs. death in slasher films: A content analysis. *Sex Roles, 23*, 187–196.

Cowlishaw, G. (2013). Reproducing criminality: How cure enhances cause. In K. Carrington, M. Ball, E. O'Brien, & J.M. Tauri (Eds.), *Crime, justice and social democracy: International perspectives* (pp. 234–247). New York: Palgrave Macmillan.

Cozens, P.M., Saville, G., & Hillier, D. (2005). Crime prevention through environmental design (CPTED): A review and modern bibliography. *Property Management, 23*, 328–356.

Cunneen, C. (2001). *Conflict, politics and crime in aboriginal communities and the police*. Sydney, Australia: Allen and Unwin.

Cunneen, C. (2007). Crime, justice and indigenous people. In E. Barclay, J.F. Donnermeyer, J. Scott, & R. Hogg (Eds.), *Crime in rural Australia* (pp. 142–153). Annandale, NSW, Australia: Federation Press.

Cupitt, M. (1997). Identifying and addressing the issues of elder abuse: A rural perspective. *Journal of Elder Abuse and Neglect, 8*, 21–30.

Currie, E. (1985). *Confronting crime: An American challenge*. New York: Pantheon.

Currie, E. (1992). Retreatism, minimalism, realism: Three styles of reasoning on crime and drugs in the United States. In J. Lowman & B.D. MacLean (Eds.), *Realist criminology: Crime control and policing in the 1990s* (pp. 88–97). Toronto: University of Toronto Press.

Currie, E. (2007). Against marginality: Arguments for a public criminology. *Theoretical Criminology, 11*, 175–190.

Currie, E. (2009). *The roots of danger: Violent crime in global perspective*. Upper Saddle River, NJ: Prentice Hall.

Currie, E. (2013). The sustaining society. In K. Carrington, M. Ball, E. O'Brien, & J.M. Tauri (Eds.), *Crime, justice and social democracy: International perspectives* (pp. 3–15). New York: Palgrave Macmillan.

Daly, K., & Chesney-Lind, M. (1988). Feminism and criminology. *Justice Quarterly, 5*, 497–538.

Danbon, D.B. (1991). Romantic agrarianism in 20th-century America. *Agricultural History, 65*, 1–12.

Davenport, J., III, & Davenport, J.A. (1984). Theoretical perspectives on rural/urban differences. *Human Services in the Rural Environment, 9*, 4–9.

Dean, A. (2002). History, culture, and substance use in a rural Scottish community. *Substance Use and Misuse, 37*, 749–766.

Dees, M. & Fiffer, S. (2001). *A lawyer's journey: The Morris Dees story*. Chicago: The American Bar Association.

Deflem, M. (1999). Ferdinand Tönnies on crime and society: An unexplored contribution to criminological sociology. *History of the Social Sciences, 12*, 87–116.

DeKeseredy, W.S. (1990). Male peer support and woman abuse: The current stake of knowledge. *Sociological Focus, 23*, 129–139.

DeKeseredy, W.S. (2007a). Review of Elliott Curries' *The road to whatever. Critical Criminology, 15*, 199–201.

DeKeseredy, W.S. (2007b). *Sexual assault during and after separation/divorce: An exploratory study.* Washington, DC: U.S. Department of Justice.

DeKeseredy, W.S. (2009). Canadian crime control in the new millennium: The influence of neo-conservative policies and practices. *Police Practice and Research, 10*, 305–316.

DeKeseredy, W.S. (2011a). *Contemporary critical criminology.* London: Routledge.

DeKeseredy, W.S. (2011b). *Violence against women: Myths, facts, controversies.* Toronto: University of Toronto Press.

DeKeseredy, W.S. (2012). The current condition of criminological theory in North America. In S. Hall & S. Winlow (Eds.), *New directions in criminological theory* (pp. 66–79). London: Routledge.

DeKeseredy, W.S. (2013). The myth that "criminals" are fundamentally different from noncriminals. In R.M. Bohm & J.T. Walker (Eds.), *Demystifying crime and criminal justice* (2nd ed., pp. 13–24). New York: Oxford University Press.

DeKeseredy, W.S. (in press). Patriarchy.com: Adult Internet pornography and the abuse of women. In C.M. Renzetti & R. Bergen (Eds.), *Understanding diversity: Celebrating difference, challenging inequality.* Boston: Allyn & Bacon.

DeKeseredy, W.S., & Donnermeyer, J.F. (2013). Thinking critically about rural crime: Toward the development of a new left realist perspective. In S. Winlow & R. Atkinson (Eds.), *New directions in crime and deviancy* (pp. 206–222). London: Routledge.

DeKeseredy, W.S., & Dragiewicz, M. (2012a). Introduction. In W.S. DeKeseredy & M. Dragiewicz (Eds.), *Routledge handbook of critical criminology* (pp. 1–8). London: Routledge.

DeKeseredy, W.S., & Dragiewicz, M. (Eds.). (2012b). *Routledge handbook of critical criminology.* London: Routledge.

DeKeseredy, W.S., & Goff, C. (1992). Corporate violence against Canadian women: Assessing left realist research and policy. *The Journal of Human Justice, 4*, 55–70.

DeKeseredy, W.S., & Hinch, R. (1991). *Woman abuse: Sociological perspectives.* Toronto: Thompson Educational Publishing.

DeKeseredy, W.S., & Joseph, C. (2006). Separation/divorce sexual assault in rural Ohio: Preliminary results of an exploratory study. *Violence Against Women, 12*, 301–311.

DeKeseredy, W.S., & MacLeod, L. (1997). *Woman abuse: A sociological story.* Toronto: Harcourt Brace.

DeKeseredy, W.S., & Olsson, P. (2011). Adult pornography, male peer support, and violence against women: The contribution of the "dark side" of the Internet. In M. Vargas Martin, M.A. Garcia Ruiz, & A. Edwards (Eds.), *Technology for facilitating humanity and combating social deviations: Interdisciplinary perspectives* (pp. 34–50). Hershey, PA: Information Science Reference.

DeKeseredy, W.S., & Rennison, C.M. (2013). Comparing female victims of male perpetrated separation/divorce assault across geographical regions: Results from the national crime victimization survey. *International Journal for Crime and Justice, 2,* 65–81.

DeKeseredy, W.S., & Schwartz, M.D. (1996). *Contemporary criminology.* Belmont, CA: Wadsworth.

DeKeseredy, W.S., & Schwartz, M.D. (1998). *Woman abuse on campus: Results from the Canadian national survey.* Thousand Oaks, CA: Sage.

DeKeseredy, W.S., & Schwartz, M.D. (2002). Theorizing public housing woman abuse as a function of economic exclusion and male peer support. *Women's Health and Urban Life, 1,* 26–45.

DeKeseredy, W.S., & Schwartz, M.D. (2006). Left realist theory. In S. Henry & M.M. Lanier (Eds.), *The essential criminology reader* (pp. 307–315). Cambridge, MA: Westview.

DeKeseredy, W.S., & Schwartz, M.D. (2008). Separation/divorce sexual assault in rural Ohio: Survivors' perceptions. *Journal of Preventions and Interventions in the Community, 36,* 105–119.

DeKeseredy, W.S., & Schwartz, M.D. (2009). *Dangerous exits: Escaping abusive relationships in rural America.* New Brunswick, NJ: Rutgers University Press.

DeKeseredy, W.S., & Schwartz, M.D. (2012). Left realism. In W.S. DeKeseredy & M. Dragiewicz (Eds.), *Routledge handbook of critical criminology* (pp. 105–116). London: Routledge.

DeKeseredy, W.S., & Schwartz, M.D. (2013). *Male peer support and violence against women: The history and verification of a theory.* Boston: Northeastern University Press.

DeKeseredy, W.S., Donnermeyer, J.F., & Schwartz, M.D. (2009). Toward a gendered second generation CPTED for preventing woman abuse in rural communities. *Security Journal, 22,* 178–189.

DeKeseredy, W.S., Ellis, D., & Alvi, S. (2005). *Deviance and crime: Theory, research and policy.* Cincinnati: LexisNexis.

DeKeseredy, W.S., Muzzatti, S.L., & Donnermeyer, J.F. (2013). Mad men in bib overalls: Media's horrification and pornification of rural culture. *Critical Criminology.* http://link.springer.com.proxy.lib.ohio-state.edu/content/pdf/10.1007%2Fs10612-013-9190-7.pdf

DeKeseredy, W.S., Rogness, M., & Schwartz, M.D. (2004). Separation/divorce sexual assault: The current state of social scientific knowledge. *Aggression and Violent Behavior, 9*, 675–691.

DeKeseredy, W.S., Schwartz, M.D., & Alvi, S. (2000). The role of profeminist men in dealing with woman abuse on the Canadian college campus. *Violence Against Women, 6*, 918–935.

DeKeseredy, W.S., Alvi, S., Renzetti, C.M., & Schwartz, M.D. (2004). Reducing private violence against women in public housing: Can second generation CPTED make a difference? *CPTED Journal, 3*, 27–37.

DeKeseredy, W.S., Alvi, S. Schwartz, M.D., & Tomaszewski, E.A. (2003). *Under siege: Poverty and crime in a public housing community*. Lanham, MD: Lexington Books.

DeKeseredy, W.S., Schwartz, M.D., Fagen, D., & Hall, M. (2006). Separation/divorce sexual assault: The contribution of male peer support. *Feminist Criminology, 1*, 228–250.

DeKeseredy, W.S., Donnermeyer, J.F., Schwartz, M.D., Tunnell, K.D., & Hall, M. (2007). Thinking critically about rural gender relations: Toward a rural masculinity crisis/male peer support model of separation/divorce sexual assault. *Critical Criminology, 15*, 295–311.

Deller, S.C., & Deller, M.A. (2010). Rural crime and social capital. *Growth and Change, 41*, 221–275.

Department of Justice, Canada. (2013). *Firearms, accidental deaths, suicides and violent crime: An updated review of the literature with special reference to the Canadian situation*. Retrieved January 8, 2013, from www.justice.gc.ca/eng/pi/rs/rep-rap/1998/wd98_4-dt98_4/p2.html.

Dimah, K.P., & Dimah, A. (2004). Elder abuse and neglect among rural and urban women. *Journal of Elder Abuse and Neglect, 15*, 75–93.

Dines, G. (2010). *Pornland: How porn has hijacked our sexuality*. Boston: Beacon Press.

Dingwall, G.,& Moody, S.R. (Eds.) (1999), *Crime and conflict in the countryside*. Cardiff: University of Wales Press.

Dinitz, S. (1973). Progress, crime, and the folk ethic: Portrait of a small town. *Criminology, 11*, 3–21.

Dobash, R.E., Dobash, R.P., Cavanagh, K., & Medina-Ariza, J. (2007). Lethal and nonlethal violence against an intimate female partner: Comparing male murderers to nonlethal abusers. *Violence Against Women, 13*, 329–353.

Donnermeyer, J.F. (1992). The use of alcohol, marijuana, and hard drugs by rural adolescents: A review of recent research. In R.W. Edwards (Ed.), *Drug use in rural American communities* (pp. 31–75). Binghampton, NY: Harrington Park Press.

Donnermeyer, J.F. (1994). Crime and violence in rural communities. In J. Blaser (Ed.), *Perspectives on violence and substance use in rural America* (pp. 27–64). Oak Brook, IL: Midwest Regional Center for Drug-Free Schools and Communities.

Donnermeyer, J.F. (1997). The economic and social costs of drug abuse among the rural population. In E.B. Robertson, Z. Sloboda, G.M. Boyd, L. Beatty, & N.J. Kozel (Eds.), *Rural substance use: State of knowledge and issues* (pp. 220–245). Rockville, MD: National Institutes of Health. NIDA Research Monograph 168.

Donnermeyer, J.F. (2007a). Locating rural crime: The role of theory. In J. Scott, R. Hogg, E. Barclay, & J. Donnermeyer (Eds.), *Crime in Rural Australia* (pp. 15–26). Annandale, NSW, Australia: Federation Press.

Donnermeyer, J.F. (2007b). Rural crime: Roots and restoration. *International Journal of Rural Crime, 1*, 2–20.

Donnermeyer, J.F. (2012). Rural crime and critical criminology. In W.S. DeKeseredy & M. Dragiewicz (Eds.), *Routledge handbook of critical criminology* (pp. 289–301). London: Routledge.

Donnermeyer, J.F., & DeKeseredy, W.S. (2008). Toward a rural critical criminology. *Southern Rural Sociology, 23*, 4–28.

Donnermeyer, J.F., & Phillips, G.H. (1984). Vandals and vandalism in the rural U.S.A. In C. Levi-Leboyer (Ed.), *Vandalism: Motivations and behaviour* (pp. 124–146). Amsterdam: North-Holland Press.

Donnermeyer, J.F., & Scheer, S.D. (2001). An analysis of substance use among adolescents from smaller places. *Journal of Rural Heath, 17*, 105–113.

Donnermeyer, J.F., & Tunnell, K. (2007). In our own backyard: Methamphetamine manufacturing, trafficking and abuse in rural America. *Rural Realities, 2*(2). Online at www.ruralsociology.org/wp-content/uploads/2012/03/Rural-Realities-2-2.pdf.

Donnermeyer, J.F., Barclay, E., & Jobes, P.C. (2013). Social disorganization, conflict and crime in four rural Australian communities. *International Journal of Rural Criminology, 2*.

Donnermeyer, J.F., Barclay, E., & Mears, D.P. (2011). Policing agricultural crime. In R.I. Mawby & R. Yarwood (Eds.), *Rural policing and policing the rural: A constable countryside?* (pp. 193–204). Farnham, UK: Ashgate.

Donnermeyer, J.F., DeKeseredy, W.S., & Dragiewicz, M. (2011). Policing rural Canada and the United States. In R.I. Mawby & R. Yarwood (Eds.), *Rural policing and policing the rural: A constable countryside?* (pp. 23–32). Farnham, UK: Ashgate.

Donnermeyer, J.F., Jobes, P., & Barclay, E. (2006). Rural crime, poverty, and community. In W.S. DeKeseredy & B. Perry (Eds.), *Advancing critical criminology: Theory and application* (pp. 199–218). Lanham, MD: Lexington Books.

Donnermeyer, J.F., Jobes, P., & Barclay, E. (2009). Sociological theory, social change, and crime in rural communities. In A. Denis & D. Kalekin-Fishman

(Eds.), *The ISA handbook in contemporary sociology: Conflict, competition, cooperation* (pp. 305–320). Los Angeles: Sage.

Donnermeyer, J.F., Oetting, E.R., Plested, B.A., Edwards, R.W., Jumper-Thurman, R., & Littlethunder, L. (1997). Community readiness and prevention programs. *Journal of the Community Development Society, 28*, 65–83.

Drake, D. (2011). The "dangerous other" in maximum-security prisons. *Criminology and Criminal Justice, 11*, 367–382.

Draus, P.J., & Carlson, R.G. (2006). Needles in the haystacks: The social context of initiation to heroin injection in rural Ohio. *Substance Use and Misuse, 41*, 1111–1124.

Dukes, R.L., & Stein, J.A. (2003). Gender and gang membership: A contrast of rural and urban youth on attitudes and behavior. *Youth and Society, 34*, 415–440.

Durkheim, E. (1964). *The division of labor in society*. New York: Free Press.

Edleman, B. (2009). Red light states: Who buys online adult entertainment? *Journal of Economic Perspectives, 23*, 209–220.

Edwards, R.W. (Ed.) (1992). *Drug use in rural communities*. Binghamton, NY: Harrington Park Press.

Edwards, R.W., & Donnermeyer, J.F. (2002). Introduction: Substance use in rural communities around the world. *Substance Use and Misuse, 37*, vii–xii.

Edwards, R.W., Jumper-Thurman, P., Plested, B.A., Oetting, E.R., & Swanson, L. (2000). Community readiness: Research to practice. *Journal of Community Psychology, 28*, 291–307.

Eller, R.D. (2008). *Uneven ground: Appalachia since 1945*. Lexington: University of Kentucky Press.

Ellis, D. (1987). *The wrong stuff: An introduction to the sociological study of deviance*. Toronto: Collier Macmillan.

Ellis, D., & DeKeseredy, W.S. (1997). Rethinking estrangement, interventions and intimate femicide. *Violence Against Women, 3*, 590–609.

Engler, R. (1986, January). Political power aids health and safety. *These Times*, 15–21.

Esselstyn, T.C. (1953). The social role of the country sheriff. *Journal of Criminal Law, Criminology, and Police Science, 44*, 177–184.

Evans, W.P., Fitzgerald, C., Weigel, D., & Chvilicek, S. (1999). Are rural gang members similar to their urban peers? Implications for rural communities. *Youth and Society, 30*, 267–282.

Feldhusen, J.F., Thurston, J.R., & Ager, E. (1965). Delinquency proneness of urban and rural youth. *Journal of Research in Crime and Delinquency, 2*, 32–44.

Feldman, T. (2004, September). Quilts for change. *Quiltations*, 4.

Felson, M. (2006). *Crime and nature*. Thousand Oaks, CA: Sage.

Felson, M., & Bora, R. (2010). *Crime and everyday life* (4th ed.). Thousand Oaks, CA: Sage.

Ferdinand, T.N. (1964). The offense patterns and family structure of urban, village and rural delinquents. *Journal of Criminal Law, Criminology, and Police Science, 55*, 86–93.

Ferrell, J., Hayward, K., & Young, J. (2008). *Cultural criminology: An invitation.* London: Sage.

Fischer, C. (1980). The spread of violent crime from city to countryside, 1955 to 1975. *Rural Sociology, 45*, 416–434.

Fischer, C. (1995). The subcultural theory of urbanism: A twenty-five year assessment. *American Journal of Sociology, 101*, 543–577.

Fisher, S.L. (1993). *Fighting back in Appalachia: Traditions of resistance and change.* Philadelphia, PA: Temple University Press.

Forsyth, C.J. (2008). The game of wardens and poachers. *Southern Rural Sociology, 23*, 43–53.

Forsyth, C.J., Gramling, R., & Wooddell, G. (1998). The game of poaching: Folk crimes in southwest Louisiana. *Society and Natural Resources, 11*, 25–38.

Foster, G.S., & Hummel, R.L. (1997). Wham, bam, thank you, Sam: Critical dimensions of the persistence of hillbilly caricatures. *Sociological Spectrum, 17*, 157–176.

Frank, R. (2003). When bad things happen in good places: Pastoralism in big-city newspaper coverage of small-town violence. *Rural Sociology, 68*, 207–230.

Freudenburg, W.R. (2006). Environmental degradation, dispproportionality, and the double diversion: Reaching out, reaching ahead, and reaching beyond. *Rural Sociology, 71*, 3–32.

Freudenburg, W.R., & Jones, R.E. (1991). Criminal behavior and rapid community growth: Examining the evidence. *Rural Sociology, 56*, 619–645.

Friedmann, H. (1993). The political economy of food: A global crisis. *New Left Review, 197*, 29–57.

Friedrichs, D.O. (2009). Critical criminology. In J.M. Miller (Ed.), *Twenty-first century criminology: A reference handbook* (vol. 1, pp. 210–218). Thousand Oaks, CA: Sage.

Friedrichs, D.O., & Rothe, D.L. (2012). Crimes of the powerful: White-collar crime and beyond. In W.S. DeKeseredy & M. Dragiewicz (Eds.), *Routledge handbook of critical criminology* (pp. 241–251). London: Routledge.

Funk, R.E. (1993). *Stopping rape: A challenge for men.* Philadelphia, PA: New Society Publishers.

Funk, R.E. (2006). *Reaching men: Strategies for preventing sexist attitudes, behaviors, and violence.* Indianapolis, IN: JIST Life.

Gagne, P.L. (1992). Appalachian women: Violence and social control. *Journal of Contemporary Ethnography, 20*, 387–415.

Gagne, P.L. (1996). Identity, strategy, and identity politics: Clemency for battered women who kill. *Social Problems, 43*, 77–93.

Gallup-Black, A. (2005). Twenty years of rural and urban trends in family and intimate partner homicide. *Homicide Studies, 9*, 149–173.

Gans, H.J. (1972). The positive functions of poverty. *American Journal of Sociology, 78*, 275–289.

Garfinkle, H. (1956). Conditions of successful degradation ceremonies. *American Journal of Sociology, 61*, 420–424.

Garland, D. (1996). The limits of the sovereign state: Strategies of crime control in contemporary society. *British Journal of Criminology, 36*, 445–471.

Garriott, W. (2011). *Policing methamphetamine: Narcopolitics in rural America.* New York: New York University Press.

Gelsthorpe, L., & Morris, A. (1988). Feminism and criminology in Britain. *British Journal of Criminology, 28*, 93–110.

Gfroerer, J.C., Larson, S.L., & Colliver, J.D. (2007). Drug use patterns and trends in rural communities. *Journal of Rural Health, 23* (supplemental issue), 10–15.

Gibbons, D.C. (1972). Crime in the hinterlands. *Criminology, 10*, 177–191.

Gibbs, J.C. (2010). Looking at terrorism through left realist lenses. *Crime, Law and Social Change, 54*, 171–185.

Gilligan, J. (2001). *Preventing violence.* New York: Thames and Hudson.

Godenzi, A., Schwartz, M.D., & DeKeseredy, W.S. (2001). Toward a gendered social bond/male peer support theory of university woman abuse. *Critical Criminology, 10*, 1–16.

Gold, D., Lo, C., & Wright, E.O. (1975). Recent developments in Marxist theories of the capitalist state. *Monthly Review, 27*, 29–51.

Gordon, D. (1971). Class and the economics of crime. *Review of Radical Political Economics, 3*, 51–75.

Grant, J. (2008). *Charting women's journeys: From addiction to recovery.* Lanham, MD: Lexington.

Grant, J. (2012). *Men and substance abuse: Narratives of addiction and recovery.* Boulder, CO: First Forum Press.

Gray, D. (2007). Foreword. In E. Barclay, J.F. Donnermeyer, J. Scott, & R. Hogg (Eds.), *Crime in rural Australia* (pp. v–vi). Annandale, NSW, Australia: Federation Press.

Greenberg, D. (Ed.). (1981). *Crime and capitalism: Readings in a Marxist criminology.* Palo Alto, CA: Mayfield.

Gunter, V., & Kroll-Smith, S. (2007). *Volatile places: A sociology of communities and environmental controversies.* Thousand Oaks, CA: Pine Forge Press.

Haight, W., Jacobsen, T., Black, J., Kingery, L., Sheridan, K., & Mulder, C. (2005). "In these bleak days": Parent methamphetamine abuse and child welfare in the rural Midwest. *Children and Youth Services Review, 27*, 949–971.

Hall, S., & Jefferson, T. (Eds.). (1977). *Resistance through rituals: Youth subcultures in post-war Britain*. London: Hutchinson & Co.

Hallsworth, S., & Lea, J. (2011). Reconstructing Leviathan: Emerging contours of the security state. *Theoretical Criminology, 15*, 141–157.

Hardesty, J.J. (2002) Separation assault in the context of postdivorce parenting: An integrative review of the literature. *Violence Against Women, 8*, 597–621.

Hardman, D. (1996). Small town gangs. *Journal of Criminal Law, Criminology and Police Science, 60*, 173–181.

Harper, T. (2013, January 11). "Tipping point is now," Atleo declares. *Toronto Star*, p. A6.

Havens, J.R., Oser, C.B., Knudsen, H.K., Lofwall, M., Stoops, W.W., Walsh, S.I., Leukefeld, C.G., & Kral, A.H. (2011). Individual and network factors associated with non-fatal overdose among rural Appalachian drug users. *Drug and Alcohol Dependence, 115*, 107–112.

Hay, D.A., & Basran, G.S. (1992). Introduction. In D.A. Hay & G.S. Basran (Eds.), *Rural sociology in Canada* (pp. ix–x). Toronto: Oxford University Press.

Hayes-Smith, J., & Whaley, R.B. (2009). Community characteristics and methamphetamine use: A social disorganization perspective. *Journal of Drug Issues, 39*, 547–576.

Hazler, R. (1996). *Breaking the cycle of violence: Interventions for bullying and victimization*. Washington, DC: Accelerated Development.

Hedayati, H. (2008). Commercial and farm vehicle theft in urban and rural Australia. *Southern Rural Sociology, 23*, 54–77.

Hirschi, T. (1969). *Causes of delinquency*. Berkeley: University of California Press.

Hobbs, F., & Stoops, N. (2002). *Demographic trends in the 20th century*. Washington, DC: U.S. Government Printing Office.

Hogg, R., & Carrington, K. (2003). Violence, spatiality and other rurals. *Australian and New Zealand Journal of Criminology, 36*, 293–319.

Hogg, R., & Carrington, R. (2006). *Policing the rural crisis*. Annandale, NSW, Australia: Federation Press.

Hornosty, J., & Doherty, D. (2002). *Responding to wife abuse in farm and rural communities: Searching for solutions that work* (SIPP Public Policy Paper 10). Fredericton, New Brunswick: Muriel McQueen Fergusson Centre for Family Violence Research.

Horwitz, J. (2013). The truth about gun sales. *Huff Post – Politics*. Retrieved March 12, 2013, from www.huffingtonpost.com/josh-horwitz/the-truth-about-gun-sales_b_1193498.html.

Hotez, P.J. (2011). America's most distressed areas and their neglected infections: The United States gulf coast and the District of Columbia. *PLOS*

Neglected Tropical Diseases. Retrieved September 7, 2012, from www.ncbi. nlm.nih.gov/pmc/articles/PMC3066143/.

Howlett, D. (2012). Sex shops infiltrate small towns. *USA Today.* Retrieved September 11, 2012, from www.usatoday.com/news/nation/2003–12–03-adultbooks-usat_x.htm.

Huff, R. (ed.). (1996). *Gangs in America.* Newbury Park, CA: Sage.

Hunt, N. (2012). Rural Canada more dangerous than our cities. Retrieved December 5, 2012, from http://news.sympatico.ca/oped/coffee-talk/rural_canada_more_dangerous_than_our_cities...

Hunter, B. (1999). *Three nations, not one: Indigenous and other Australian poverty* (CAEPR Working Paper No. 1). Australian National University.

Inge, T.D. (1989). Comic strips. In C.R. Wilson & W. Ferris (Eds.), *Encyclopedia of southern culture* (pp. 914–915). Chapel Hill: University of North Carolina Press.

Ingram, A.L. (1993). Type of place, urbanism, and delinquency: Further testing the determinist theory. *Journal of Research on Crime and Delinquency, 30*, 192–212.

Ireland, T.O., Thornberry, T.P., & Loeber, R. (2003). Violence among adolescents living in public housing: A two site analysis. *Criminology and Public Policy, 3*, 3–38.

Irwin, J. (1985, November). *The return of the bogeyman.* Keynote address at American Society of Criminology, San Diego, CA.

Jacobs, J. (2005). *Dark age ahead.* Toronto: Vintage Canada.

Jaggar, A. (1983). *Feminist politics and human nature.* Totowa, NJ: Rowman & Littlefield.

Jensen, L. (2006). At the razor's edge: Building hope for America's rural poor. *Rural Realities, 1*, 1–8.

Jensen, R. (2007). *Getting off: Pornography and the end of masculinity.* Cambridge, MA: South End Press.

Jewkes, R., Dunkle, K., Koss, M.P., Levin, J.B., Nduna, M., Jama, N., & Sikweyiya, Y. (2006). Rape perpetration by young, rural South African men: Prevalence, patterns and risk factors. *Social Science and Medicine, 63*, 2929–2961.

Jobes, P.C. (1999). Residential stability and crime in small rural agricultural and recreational towns. *Sociological Perspectives, 42*, 499–524.

Jobes, P.C. (2002). Effective officer and good neighbour: Problems and perceptions among police in rural Australia. *Policing, 25*, 256–273.

Jobes, P.C. (2003). Human ecology and rural policing: A grounded theoretical analysis of how personal constraints and community characteristics influence strategies of law enforcement in rural New South Wales, Australia. *Police Practices and Research, 4*, 3–19.

Jobes, P.C., Donnermeyer, J.F., & Barclay, E. (2005). A tale of two towns: Social structure, integration and crime in rural New South Wales. *Sociologia Ruralis, 45,* 224–244.

Jobes, P.C., Barclay, E., Weinand, H., & Donnermeyer, J. F. (2004). A structural analysis of social disorganization and crime in rural communities in Australia. *Australian and New Zealand Journal of Criminology, 37,* 114–140.

Johnson, K. (2006). *Demographic trends in rural and small town America.* Durham: University of New Hampshire, Carsey Institute.

Johnson, M.P. (1995). Patriarchal violence and common couple violence: Two forms of violence against women. *Journal of Marriage and the Family, 57,* 283–294.

Johnston, L.D., O'Malley, P.M., Bachman, J.G., & Schulenberg, J.E. (2012). *Monitoring the future: National survey results on drug use, 1975–2011: Vol. 1. Secondary school students.* Ann Arbor: University of Michigan, Institute for Social Research.

Kappeler, V.E., & Potter, G.W. (2005). *The mythology of crime and criminal justice* (4th ed.). Long Grove, IL: Waveland Press.

Katz, J. 2006. *The macho paradox: Why some men hurt women and how all men can help.* Naperville, IL: Sourcebooks.

Kay, B. (2011). *The urban–rural factor.* Waterloo, ON: Laurier Institute for the Study of Public Opinion and Policy.

Kaylen, M.T. (2010). *A test of three methodological explanations for inconsistencies in rural social disorganization and youth violence research* (master's thesis). Indiana University, Department of Criminal Justice.

Kaylen, M.T., & Pridemore, W.A. (2011). A reassessment of the association between social disorganization and youth violence in rural areas. *Social Science Quarterly, 92,* 978–1001.

Kaylen, M.T., & Pridemore, W.A. (2012). Systematically addressing inconsistencies in the rural social disorganization and crime literature. *International Journal of Rural Criminology, 1,* 134–152.

Kaylen, M.T., & Pridemore, W.A. (2013). The association between social disorganization and rural violence is sensitive to the measurement of the dependent variable. *Criminal Justice Review,* 13 February. online at http://cjr.sagepub.com/content/early/2013/02/11/0734016813476715

Kelleher, K.J., & Robbins, J.M. (1997). Social and economic consequences of rural alcohol use. In E.B. Robertson, Z. Sloboda, G.M. Boyd, L. Beatty, & N.J. Kozel (Eds.), *Rural substance use: State of knowledge and issues* (pp. 196–119). Rockville, MD: National Institutes of Health. NIDA Research Monograph 168.

Kennedy, R. (1997). *Race, crime, and the law.* New York: Vintage Books.

Kimmel, M., & Ferber, A.L. (2000). "White men are this nation": Right-wing militias and the restoration of rural American masculinity. *Rural Sociology, 65*, 582–604.

Kimmel, M.S., & Mosmiller, T.E. (1992). Introduction. In M.S. Kimmel & T.E. Mosmiller (Eds.), *Against the tide: Pro-feminist men in the United States, 1776–1990* (pp. 1–46). Boston: Beacon Press.

King, S. (1981). *Danse macabre.* New York: Berkley.

Kirkwood, C. (1993). *Leaving abusive partners.* Newbury Park, CA: Sage.

Klassen, T. (2013). The rise of South Korea and lessons for Canada. *thestar.com.* Retrieved January 11, 2013, from www.thestar.com/opinion/editorialopin-ion/article1311799–the-rise-of-sourth-korea.

Kowalski, G.S., & Duffield, D. (1990). The impact of the rural population component on homicide rates in the United States: A county-level analysis. *Rural Sociology, 55*, 76–90.

Krannich, R.S., & Petrzelka, P. (2003). Tourism and natural amenity develop-ment. In D.L. Brown & L.E. Swanson (Eds.), *Challenges for rural America in the 21st century* (pp. 190–199). University Park: Pennsylvania State Univer-sity Press.

Krannich, R.S., Berry, E.H., & Greider, T. (1989). Fear of crime in rapidly changing rural communities: A longitudinal analysis. *Rural Sociology, 54*, 195–212.

Krannich, R.S., Greider, T., & Little, R.L. (1985). Rapid growth and fear of crime: A four-community comparison. *Rural Sociology, 50*, 195–209.

Kraska, P.B., & Cubellis, L.J. (1997). Militarizing Mayberry and beyond: Making sense of American paramilitary policing. *Justice Quarterly, 14*, 607–629.

Krishnan, S. (2005). Do structural inequalities contribute to marital violence? Ethnographic evidence from rural south India. *Violence Against Women, 11*, 759–775.

Krishnan, S.P., Hilbert, J.C., & Pace, M. (2001). An examination of intimate partner violence in rural communities: Results from a hospital emergency department study from southwest United States. *Family Community Health, 24*, 1–14.

Kristof, N.D. (2012, December 23). Do we have courage? *New York Times International Weekly*, p. 15.

Kubrin, C.E. (2009). Social disorganization theory: Then, now, and in the future. In M.D. Krohn, A.J. Lizotte, & G.P. Hall (Eds.), *Handbook on crime and deviance* (pp. 225–236). New York: Springer.

Kuperan, K., & Sutenin, J.G. (1998). Blue water crime: Deterrence, legitimacy and compliance in fisheries. *Law and Society Review, 32*, 309–330.

Lab, S.P. (2003). Let's put it into context. *Criminology and Public Policy, 3*, 39–44.

Lagey, J.C. (1957). The ecology of juvenile delinquency in the small city and the rural hinterland. *Rural Sociology, 22,* 230–234.

Laub, J.H. (1983). Patterns of offending in urban and rural areas. *Journal of Criminal Justice, 11,* 129–142.

Lea, J., & Young, J. (1984). *What is to be done about law and order?* New York: Penguin.

Leach, F. (2006). Researching gender violence in schools: Methodological and ethical considerations. *World Development, 34,* 1129–1147.

Lee, M.R. (1997, April 2). Watch who you're calling "trailer trash." *Chicago Tribune,* p. 11.

Lee, M.R. (2006). The religious institutional base and violent crime in rural areas. *Journal for the Scientific Study of Religion, 45,* 309–324.

Lee, M.R. (2008). Civic community in the hinterland: Toward a theory of rural social structure and violence. *Criminology, 46,* 447–478.

Lee, M.R., & Bartkowski, J.P. (2004a). Civic participation, regional subcultures, and violence: The differential effects of secular and religious participation on adult and juvenile homicide. *Homicide Studies, 8,* 5–39.

Lee, M.R., & Bartkowski, J.P. (2004b). Love thy neighbor? Moral communities, civic engagement, and juvenile homicide in non-metro communities. *Social Forces, 82,* 1001–1035.

Lee, M.R., & Ousey, G.C. (2001). Size matters: Examining the link between small manufacturing, socioeconomic deprivation, and crime rates in nonmetropolitan communities. *Sociological Quarterly, 42,* 581–602.

Lee, M.R., & Slack, T. (2008). Labor market conditions and violent crime across the metro–nometro divide. *Social Science Research, 37,* 753–768.

Lee, M.R., & Stevenson, G.D. (2006). Gender-specific homicide offending in rural areas. *Homicide Studies, 10,* 55–73.

Lee, M.R., & Thomas, S.A. (2010). Civic community, population change, and violent crime in rural communities. *Journal of Research on Crime and Delinquency, 47,* 118–147.

Lee, M.R., Maume, M.O., & Ousey,G.C. (2003). Social isolation and lethal violence across the metro-non-metro divide: The effects of socioeconomic disadvantage and poverty concentration on homicide. *Rural Sociology, 68,* 107–131.

Lemann, N. (1991). *The promised land: The great black migration and how it changed America.* New York, Alfred A. Knopf.

Lentz, W.P. (1956). Rural–urban differentials and juvenile delinquency. *Journal of Criminal Law, Criminology and Police Science, 47,* 331–339.

Leukefeld, C.G., Logan, T.K., Farabee, D., & Clayton, R. (2002). Drug use and AIDS: Estimating injection prevalence in a rural state. *Substance Use and Misuse, 37,* 767–782.

Lewis, S.H. (2003). *Unspoken crimes: Sexual assault in rural America*. Enola, PA: National Sexual Violence Resource Center.

Li, Y.Y. (2012). Social structure and informal social control in rural communities. *International Journal of Rural Criminology, 1,* 63–88.

Lichter, D.T., & Brown, D.L. (2011). Rural America in an urban society: Changing spatial and social boundaries. *Annual Review of Sociology, 37,* 1–28.

Lichter, S.R., Amundson, D., & Lichter, L. (2003). *Perceptions of rural America: Media coverage*. Washington, DC: Center for Media and Public Affairs.

Liepins, R. (2000). New energies for an old idea: Reworking approaches to "community" in contemporary rural studies. *Journal of Rural Studies, 16,* 23–35.

Linz, D., Donnerstein, E., & Penrod, S. (1984). The effects of multiple exposures to filmed violence against women. *Journal of Communication, 34,* 130–147.

Lobao, L. (2006). Gendered places and place-based gender identities: Reflections and refractions. In H. Campbell, M. Mayerfeld Bell, & M. Finney (Eds.), *Country boys: Masculinity and rural life* (pp. 267–276). University Park: Pennsylvania State University Press.

Lobao, L., & Meyer, K. (2001). The great agricultural transition: Crisis, change, and social consequences of 20th-century U.S. farming. *Annual Review of Sociology, 27,* 103–124.

Logan, J. (1996). Rural America as a symbol of American values. *Rural Development Perspectives, 12,* 24–28.

Logan, T.K., Stevenson, E., Evans, L., & Leukefeld, C. (2004). Rural and urban women's perceptions to barriers to health, mental health, and criminal justice services: Implications for victim services. *Violence and Victims, 19,* 37–62.

Longino, H. (1980). What is pornography? In L. Lederer (Ed.), *Take back the night: Women on pornography* (pp. 40–54). New York: William Morrow.

Luttwak, E. (1995, November). Turbo-charged capitalism and its consequences. *London Review of Books,* pp. 6–7.

Lyman, M.D., & Potter, G.W. (1998). *Drugs in society: Causes, concepts and control*. Cincinnati, OH: Anderson Publishing Co.

MacDowell, L. (2012). What's wrong with Caterpillar? *Our Times: Canada's Independent Labor Magazine*. Retrieved January 9, 2013, from http://ourtimes.ca/Between_Times/article_188.php.

Malamuth, N.M., & Check, J.V.P. (1981). The effects of mass media exposure on acceptance of violence against women: A field experiment. *Journal of Research in Personality, 15,* 436–446.

Malley-Morrison, K., & Hines, D.A. (2004). *Family violence in a cultural perspective: Defining, understanding, and combating abuse*. Thousand Oaks, CA: Sage.

Mamman, L.S., Brieger, W.R., & Oshiname, F.O. (2002). Alcohol consumption pattern among women in a rural Yoruba community in Nigeria. *Substance Use and Misuse, 37,* 579–598.

Mann, S.A., & Dickinson, J.M. (1978). Obstacles to the development of a capitalist agriculture. *Journal of Peasant Studies, 5,* 466–481.

Mannheim, K. (1954). *Ideology and Utopia.* New York: Harcourt, Brace.

Masters, J. (2012). *What is the fiscal cliff?* New York: Council on Foreign Relations.

Matthews, R. (2009). Beyond "so what?" criminology: Rediscovering realism. *Theoretical Criminology, 13,* 341–362.

Matthews, R.A. (2003). Marxist criminology. In M.D. Schwartz & S.E. Hatty (Eds.), *Controversies in critical criminology* (pp. 1–14). Cincinnati, OH: Anderson.

Matthews, R.A. (2012). Marxist criminology. In W.S. DeKeseredy & M. Dragiewicz (Eds.), *Routledge handbook of critical criminology* (pp. 93–104). London: Routledge.

Mawby, R.I., & Yarwood, R. (Eds.), *Rural policing and policing the rural: A constable countryside?* Farnham, UK: Ashgate.

Mazur, A.G., & McBride-Stetson, D. (1995). Conclusion: The case for state feminism. In A.G. Mazur & D. McBride-Stetson (Eds.), *Comparative state feminism* (pp. 272–291). London: Sage.

McElwee, G., Smith, R., & Somerville, P. (2011). Theorising illegal rural enterprise: Is everyone at it? *International Journal of Rural Criminology, 1,* 40–62.

McFarlane, J., & Malecha, A. (2005). *Sexual assault among intimates: Frequency, consequences, and treatments.* Washington, DC: U.S. Department of Justice.

McKinney, J.C. (1966). *Constructive typology and social theory.* New York: Appleton-Century-Crofts.

McMichael, P. (2008). *Development and social change: A global perspective* (4th ed.). Los Angeles: Pine Forge Press.

Mehling, R. (2008). *Methamphetamine.* New York: Chelsea House.

Mencken, F.C., & Barnett, C. (1999). Murder, nonnegligent manslaughter, and spatial autocorrelation in mid-south counties. *Journal of Quantitative Criminology, 15,* 407–422.

Merton, R.K. (1949). *Social theory and social structure.* New York: Free Press of Glencoe.

Messerschmidt, J.W. (1986). *Capitalism, patriarchy, and crime: Toward a socialist feminist criminology.* Totowa, NJ: Rowman & Littlefield.

Messerschmidt, J.W. (1993). *Masculinities and crime: Critique and reconceptualization.* Lanham, MD: Roman & Littlefield.

Messerschmidt, J.W. (2000). *Nine lives: Adolescent masculinities, the body, and violence.* Boulder, CO: Westview.

Michalowski, R.J. (1983, Summer). Crime control in the 1980s: A progressive agenda. *Crime and Social Justice*, 13–23.

Michalowski, R.J. (1996). Critical criminology and the critique of domination: The story of an intellectual movement. *Critical Criminology, 1*, 9–16.

Miliband, R. (1969). *The state in capitalist society: The analysis of the western system of power*. London: Quartet.

Mills, A. (2012). *William Chambliss*. Retrieved December 20, 2012 from www.criminology.fsu.edu/crimtheory/chambliss.htm.

Mills, C.W. (1943). The professional ideology of social pathologists. *American Journal of Sociology, 49*, 165–180.

Mills, C.W. (1959). *The sociological imagination*. New York: Oxford University Press.

Moats, J.B. (2007). *Agroterrorism: A guide for first responders*. College Station: Texas A & M University.

Modleski, T. (1986). The terror of pleasure: The contemporary horror film and postmodern theory. In T. Modleski (Ed.), *Studies in entertainment: Critical approaches to mass culture* (pp. 155–166). Bloomington: University of Indiana Press.

Moody, S.R. (1999). Rural neglect: The case against criminology. In G. Dingwall & S.R. Moody (Eds.), *Crime and conflict in the countryside* (pp. 8–28). Cardiff: University of Wales Press.

Mooney, J. (2012). Finding a political voice: The emergence of critical criminology in Britain. In W.S. DeKeseredy & M. Dragiewicz (Eds.), *Routledge handbook of critical criminology* (pp. 13–31). London: Routledge.

Mooney, P.H. (1988). *My own boss? Class, rationality, and the family farm*. Boulder, CO: Westview Press.

Moss, M., & Rivera, R. (2012, December 23). Guns were part of a town that is full of pain. *New York Times International Weekly*, p. 7.

Mowlabocus, S. (2010). Porn 20? Technology, social practice, and the new online porn industry. In F. Attwood (Ed.), *Porn.com: Making sense of online pornography* (pp. 69–87). New York: Peter Lang.

Muth, R.M. (1998). The persistence of poaching in advanced industrial society: Meanings, and motivations – An introductory comment. *Society and Natural Resources, 11*, 5–7.

Muzzatti, S.L. (2012). Cultural criminology: Burning up capitalism, consumer culture. In W.S. DeKeseredy & M. Dragiewicz (Eds.), *Routledge handbook of critical criminology* (pp. 138–149). London: Routledge.

National Center for Children in Poverty (2005). *Child poverty in 21st-century America: Child poverty in states hit by Hurricane Katrina*. New York: Mailman School of Public Health, Columbia University.

National Research Council (2003). *Elder mistreatment: Abuse, neglect, and exploitation in an aging America*. Washington, DC: National Academies Press.

Navin, S., Stockum, R., & Campbell-Ruggaard, J. (1993). Battered women in rural America. *Journal of Human Educational Development, 32*, 9–16.

Nelsen, C., Corzine, J., & Huff-Corzine, L. (1994). The violent west re-examined: A research note on regional homicide rates. *Criminology, 32*, 149–161.

Ni Laoire, C., & Fielding, S. (2006). Rooted and routed masculinities among the rural youth of North Cork and Upper Swaledale. In H. Campbell, M. Mayerfeld Bell, & M. Finney (Eds.), *Country boys: Masculinity and rural life* (pp. 105–120). University Park: Pennsylvania State University Press.

Nisbett, R.E. (1993). Violence and U.S. regional culture. *American Psychologist, 48*, 441–449.

Nisbett, R.E., & Cohen, D. (1996). *Culture of honor: The psychology of violence in the South.* Boulder, CO: Westview Press.

Nolan, J.J. III. (2004). Establishing the statistical relationship between population size and UCR crime rate: Its impact and implications. *Journal of Criminal Justice, 32*, 547–555.

O'Connor, M., & Gray, D. (1989). *Crime in a rural community.* Annandale, NSW, Australia: Federation Press.

O'Dea, P.J., Murphy, B., & Balzer, C. (1997). Traffic and illegal production of drugs in rural America. In E.B. Robertson, Z. Sloboda, G.M. Boyd, L. Beatty, & N.J. Kozel (Eds.), *Rural substance use: State of knowledge and issues* (pp. 79–89). Rockville, MD: National Institutes of Health. NIDA Research Monograph 168.

Oetting, E.R., & Donnermeyer, J.F. (1998). Primary socialization theory: The etiology of drug use and deviance. *Substance Use and Misuse, 33*, 995–1026.

Oetting, E.R., Donnermeyer, J.F., & Deffenbacher, J.L. (1998). Primary socialization theory: The influence of community on drug use and deviance. III. *Substance Use and Misuse, 33*, 1629–1665.

Oetting, E.R., Edwards, R.W., Kelly, K., & Beauvais, F. (1997). Risk and protective factors for drug use among rural American youth. In E.B. Robertson, Z. Sloboda, G.M. Boyd, L. Beatty, & N.J. Kozel (Eds.), *Rural substance use: State of knowledge and issues* (pp. 90–130). Rockville, MD: National Institutes of Health. NIDA Research Monograph 168.

Osgood, D.W., & Chambers, J.M. (2000). Social disorganization outside the metropolis: An analysis of rural youth violence. *Criminology, 38*, 81–116.

Osgood, D.W., & Chambers, J.M. (2003). *Community correlates of rural youth violence.* Washington, DC: U.S. Department of Justice.

Ousey, G.C., & Lee. M.R. (2010). Whose civic community? Testing alternative hypotheses of the relationship between civic community and racial inequality in arrest rates. *Sociological Spectrum, 30*, 550–579.

Owen, S. (2012). *Integrated response policy to domestic violence in NSW: A critical analysis* (doctoral dissertation). Queensland University of Technology, School of Justice.

Panda, P., & Agarwal, B. (2005). Marital violence, human development and women's property status in India. *World Development, 33*, 823–850.

Paul, P. (2005). *Pornified: How pornography is transforming our lives, our relationships, and our families.* New York: Henry Holt.

Payne, B.K., Berg, B.L., & Sun, I.Y. (2005). Policing in small town America: Dogs, drunks, disorder, and dysfunction. *Journal of Criminal Justice, 33*, 31–41.

Pearce, F. (1976). *Crimes of the powerful: Marxism, crime and deviance.* London: Pluto Press.

Perreault, S. (2011). *Violent victimization of Aboriginal people in the Canadian provinces, 2009.* Ottawa: Statistics Canada.

Perry, B. (2001). *In the name of hate: Understanding hate crimes.* New York: Routledge.

Perry, B. (2003). Accounting for hate crime. In M.D. Schwartz & S.E. Hatty (Eds.), *Controversies in critical criminology* (pp. 147–160). Cincinnati, OH: Anderson.

Perry, B. (2009). *Policing race and place in Indian country.* Lanham, MD: Lexington.

Petee, T.A., & Kowalski, G.S. (1993). Modeling rural violent crime rates: A test of social disorganization theory. *Sociological Focus, 26*, 87–89.

Pew Research Center for the People and the Press. (2013). *Why own a gun? Protection is now top reason: Perspectives of gun owners, non-owners. Section 3: Gun ownership trends and demographics.* Retrieved March 12, 2013 from www.people-press.org/2013/03/12/section-3-gun-ownership-trends-and-demographics/

Pfeffer, M. (1984). Social origins of three systems of farm production in the United States. *Rural Sociology, 48*, 540–562.

Phillips, D.W., & Hundersmarck, S.F. (2008). Special issue editors' note. *Southern Rural Sociology, 23*, 1–3.

Philo, C. (1997). Of other rurals? In P. Cloke & J. Little (Eds.), *Contested countryside cultures: Otherness, marginalisation and rurality* (pp. 19–50). London: Routledge.

Platt, A. (1978). Street crime: A view from the left. *Crime and Social Justice, 9*, 26–34.

Polk, K. (1969). Delinquency and community action in non-metropolitan areas. In R.R. Cressey & D.A. Ward (Eds.), *Delinquency, crime and social process* (pp. 376–387). New York: Harper and Row, Publishers.

Polk, K. (2003). Masculinities, femininities and homicide: Competing explanations for male violence. In M.D. Schwartz & S.E. Hatty (Eds.), *Controversies in critical criminology* (pp. 133–146). Cincinnati, OH: Anderson.

Potter, G., & Gaines, L. (1992). Country comfort: Vice and corruption in rural settings. *Journal of Contemporary Criminal Justice, 8*, 36–61.

Potter, H. (Ed.). (2007). *Racing the storm: Racial implications and lessons learned from Hurricane Katrina*. Lanham, MD: Lexington.

Poulantzas, N. (1973). *Political power and social class*. Atlantic Fields, NJ: Humanities Press.

Pratt, L.R. (2009). The forgotten fifth: Rural youth and substance abuse. *Stanford Law and Policy Review, 20*, 359–404.

Price, R. (2002, May 10). Cheaper labor moves Rocky Shoe production to Puerto Rico. *Puerto Rico Herald*, p. 1.

Purdon, C. (2003). *Woman abuse and Ontario Works in a rural community: Rural women speak out about their experiences with Ontario Works*. Ottawa: Status of Women Canada.

Quinney, R. (1977). *Class, state and crime: On the theory and practice of criminal justice*. New York: David McKay Company.

Rapaport, E. (1994). The death penalty and the domestic discount. In M. Fineman & R. Mykitiuk (Eds.), *The public nature of private violence* (pp. 224–254). New York: Routledge.

Rawson, R.W. (1839). An inquiry into the statistics of crime in England and Wales. *Journal of the Royal Statistical Society of London, 2*, 316–344.

Ray, L. (2011). *Violence and society*. London: Sage.

Reiman, J., & Leighton, P. (2010). *The rich get richer and the poor get prison* (9th ed.). Boston: Allyn & Bacon.

Reiner, R. (2012). Political economy and criminology: The return of the repressed. In S. Hall & S. Winlow (Eds.), *New directions in criminological theory* (pp. 30–51). London: Routledge.

Reisig, M.D., & Cancino, J.M. (2004). Incivilities in non-metropolitan communities: The effects of structural constraints, social conditions, and crime. *Journal of Criminal Justice, 32*, 15–29.

Rennison, C.M., DeKeseredy, W.S., & Dragiewicz, M. (2012). Urban, suburban, and rural variations in separation/divorce rape/sexual assault: Results from the National Crime Victimization Survey. *Feminist Criminology, 7*, 282–297.

Rennison, C.M., DeKeseredy, W.S., & Dragiewicz, M. (in press). Intimate relationship status variations in violence against women: Urban, suburban, and rural differences. *Violence Against Women*.

Renzetti, C.M. (2011). Economic issues and intimate partner violence. In C.M. Renzetti, J.L. Edleson, & R.K. Bergen (Eds.), *Sourcebook on violence against women* (pp. 171–187). Thousand Oaks, CA: Sage.

Renzetti, C.M. (2012). Feminist perspectives in criminology. In W.S. DeKeseredy & M. Dragiewicz (Eds.), *Routledge handbook of criminology* (pp. 129–137). London: Routledge.

Renzetti, C.M. (2013). *Feminist criminology*. London: Routledge.

Renzetti, C.M., & Maier, S. (2002). "Private" crime in public housing: Fear of crime and violent victimization among women public housing residents. *Women's Health and Urban Life, 1*, 46–65.

Rephann, T.R. (1999). Links between rural development and crime. *Papers in Regional Science, 78*, 365–386.

Resig, M.D., & Cancino, J.M. (2004). Incivilities in non-metropolitan communities: The effects of structural constraints, social conditions, and crime. *Journal of Criminal Justice, 32*, 15–29.

Restoule, B.M. (2009). Aboriginal women and the criminal justice system. In J. Barker (Ed.), *Women and the criminal justice system: A Canadian perspective* (pp. 257–288). Toronto: Emond Montgomery.

Ritzer, G. (2013). *The McDonaldization of society*. Thousand Oaks, CA: Pine Forge Press.

Robertson, E.B., & Donnermeyer, J.F. (1997). Illegal drug use among rural adults: Mental health consequences and treatment utilization. *American Journal of Drug and Alcohol Abuse, 23*, 467–484.

Robertson, E.B., & Donnermeyer, J.F. (1998). Patterns of drug use among non-metropolitan and rural adults. *Substance Use and Misuse, 33*, 2109–2129.

Robertson, E.B., Sloboda, Z., Boyd, G.M., Beatty, L., & Kozel, N.J. (Eds.) (1997). *Rural substance use: State of knowledge and issues*. Rockville, M.D.: National Institutes of Health. NIDA Research Monograph 168

Robinson, W.S. (1950). Ecological correlations and the behavior of individuals. *American Sociological Review, 15*, 351–357.

Rockell, B.A. (2013). Women and crime in the rural-urban fringe. *International Journal of Rural Criminology, 2*, 24–45.

Rogers, S. (2012, July 22). Gun homicides and gun ownership listed by country. *Guardian*. Retrieved January 9, 2013, from www.guardian.co.uk/news/datablog/2012/jul/22/gun-homicides-ownership-world-list.

Rohrer, W.C., & Douglas, L.H. (1969). *The agrarian transition in America: Dualism and change*. Indianapolis, IN: The Bobbs-Merrill Company, Inc.

Rothenberg, D. (1998). *With these hands: The hidden world of migrant farmworkers today*. New York: Harcourt, Brace & Co.

Rotolo, T., & Tittle, C.R. (2006). Population size, change, and crime in U.S. cities. *Journal of Quantitative Criminology, 22*, 341–367.

Royal Canadian Mounted Police. (2013). *Urban and rural firearm deaths in Canada*. Retrieved January 8, 2013, from www.rcmp-grc.gc.ca/cfp-pcaf/res-rec/urb-eng.htm.

Russell, B. (1945). *A history of western philosophy*. New York: Simon & Schuster.

Russell, S. (2002). The continuing relevance of Marxism to critical criminology. *Critical Criminology, 11*, 93–112.

Rye, F.J., & Andrzejewska, J. (2010). The structural disempowerment of Eastern European farm workers in Norwegian agriculture. *Journal of Rural Studies, 26*, 41–51.

Sampson, R.J. (1987). Communities and crime. In M.R. Gottfredson & T. Hirschi (Eds.), *Positive criminology* (pp. 91–114). Newburg Park, CA: Sage.

Sampson, R.J. (2012). *Great American city: Chicago and the enduring neighborhood effect*. Chicago: University of Chicago Press.

Sampson, R.J. (2013). The place of context: A theory and strategy for criminology's hard problems. *Criminology, 51*, 1–31.

Sampson, R.J., & Groves, W.B. (1989). Community structure and crime: Testing social disorganization theory. *American Journal of Sociology, 94*, 774–802.

Sampson, R.J., Raudenbush, S.W., & Earls, F. (1998). *Neighborhood collective efficacy: Does it help reduce violence?* Washington, DC: U.S. Department of Justice.

Saville, G. (1996). *Assembling risk and crime potentials in neighbourhoods*. Paper presented at the 1st Annual International CPTED Association Conference. Calgary, Canada. October 30–November 1.

Saville, G. (2004). Editor's introduction. *CPTED Journal, 3*, 1–2.

Saville, G., & Clear, T. (2000). Community renaissance with community justice. *Neighborworks Journal, 18*, 19–24.

Scheer, S.D., Borden, L.M., & Donnermeyer, J.F. (2000). The relationship between family factors and adolescent substance use in rural, suburban and urban settings. *Journal of Child and Family Studies, 9*, 105–115.

Schmidt, C.W. (2009). Environmental crime: profiting at the earth's expense. In R. White (Ed.), *Environmental crime: A reader* (pp. 269–277). Cullompton, UK: Willan Publishing.

Schriver, T.E., & Kennedy, D.K. (2005). Contested environmental hazards and community conflict over relocation. *Rural Sociology, 70*, 491–513.

Schur, E.M. (1984). *Labeling women deviant: Gender, stigma and social control*. Philadelphia, PA: Temple University Press.

Sconce, J. (1995). "Trashing" the academy: Taste, excess, and the merging politics of cinematic style. *Screen, 36*, 371–393.

Scott, J., & Jobes, P.C. (2007). Policing of rural Australia. In E. Barclay, J.F. Donnermeyer, J. Scott, & R. Hogg (Eds.), *Crime in rural Australia* (pp. 127–137). Annandale, NSW, Australia: Federation Press.

Scott, J., Hogg, R., Barclay, E., & Donnermeyer, J.F. (2007). There's crime out there, but not as we know it: Rural criminology – the last frontier. In E. Barclay, J.F. Donnermeyer, J. Scott, & R. Hogg (Eds.), *Crime in rural Australia* (pp. 1–12). Annandale, NSW, Australia: Federation Press.

Sernau, S. (2006). *Global problems: The search for equity, peace, and sustainability*. Boston: Pearson.

Sev'er, A. (2002). *Fleeing the house of horrors: Women who have left abusive partners*. Toronto: University of Toronto Press.

Sev'er, A. (2012). Review of Walter S. DeKeseredy's *Violence against women: Myths, facts, controversies*. *Women's Health and Urban Life, 11*, 88–95.

Seydlitz, R., Laska, S., Spain, D., Triche, E.W., and Bishop, K.L. (1993). Development and social problems: The impact of the offshore oil industry on suicide and homicide rates. *Rural Sociology, 58*, 93–116.

Shaw, C.R., & McKay, H.D. (1942). *Juvenile delinquency and urban areas*. Chicago: University of Chicago Press.

Sherman, J. (2005). *Men without sawmills: Masculinity, rural poverty, and family stability*. Columbia, MO: Rural Poverty Research Center.

Sherrill, R. (2001, January 8). Death trip: The American way of execution. *Nation*. Retrieved January 25, 2010, from www.thenation.com/doc/20010108/sherrill.

Short, B. (2006). Idyllic ruralities. In P. Cloke, T. Marsden, & P.H. Mooney (Eds.), *Handbook of rural studies* (pp. 133–146). London: Sage.

Siegel, L., & McCormick, C. (2012). *Criminology in Canada: Theories, patterns, and typologies* (5th ed.). Toronto: Nelson.

Simon, S. (2004). Hard-core porn hits the heartland: Rural superstores are "doing great." *Concord Monitor*. Retrieved December 7, 2004, from www.monitor.com/apps/pbcs.dll/article?AID=/20041207/REPOSITORY/412070332/1014.

Skoog, D. (1996). Taking control: Native self-government and native policing. In M. Nielsen & R. Silverman (Eds.), *Native Americans, crime and justice* (pp. 118–131). Boulder, CO: Westview.

Slayden, D. (2010). Debbie does Dallas again and again: Pornography, technology, and market innovation. In F. Attwood (Ed.), *Porn.com: Making sense of online pornography* (pp. 54–68). New York: Peter Lang.

Smith, B. (1933). *Rural crime control*. New York: Institute of Public Administration.

Smith, M.D. (1990). Patriarchal ideology and wife beating: A test of a feminist hypothesis. *Violence and Victims, 5*, 257–273.

Sokoloff, N.J. (Ed.). (2005). *Domestic violence at the margins: Readings on race, class, gender, and culture*. New Brunswick, NJ: Rutgers University Press.

Sokoloff, N.J., & Dupont, I. (2005). Domestic violence: Examining the intersections of race, class, and gender – An introduction. In N. Sokoloff (Ed.), *Domestic violence at the margins: Readings on race, class, gender, and culture* (pp. 1–14). New Brunswick, NJ: Rutgers University Press.

Sorokin, P., Zimmerman, C., & Galpin, C. (1931). *A systematic sourcebook in rural sociology: Vol. 2*. Minneapolis: University of Minnesota Press.

South, N., & Brisman, A. (Eds.). (2013). *Routledge international handbook of green criminology*. London: Routledge.

Southern Poverty Law Center (2011).*The year in hate and extremism*. Atlanta, GA: Southern Poverty Law Center.

Spano, R., & Nagy, S. (2005). Social guardianship and social isolation: An application and extension of lifestyle/routine activities theory to rural adolescents. *Rural Sociology, 70*, 414–437.

Spitzer, S. (1975). Toward a Marxian theory of deviance. *Social Problems, 22*, 638–651.

Spitzer, S. (2008). The production of deviance in capitalist societies. In E.J. Clarke (Ed.), *Deviant behavior: A text-reader in the sociology of deviance* (7th ed., pp. 67–74). New York: Worth.

Srinivasan, S., & Bedi, A. (2007). Domestic violence and dowry: Evidence from a south Indian village. *World Development, 35*, 857–880.

Stallwitz, A. (2012). *The role of community-mindedness in the self-regulation of drug cultures: A case study from the Shetland Islands*. Dordrecht, The Netherlands: Springer.

Stallwitz, A., & Shewan, D. (2004). A qualitative exploration of the impact of cultural and social factors on heroin use in Shetland (Scotland). *Journal of Psychoactive Drugs, 36*, 367–378.

Stark, E. (2007). *Coercive control: How men entrap women in personal life*. New York: Oxford University Press.

Statistics Canada. (2005). *Social relationships in rural and urban Canada*. Ottawa: Author.

Stough-Hunter, A. (2010, October). *When health involves hunting, fishing, and peeing in the front yard: An ethnographic approach to perceptions of "healthy living" among men in western Pennsylvania*. Paper presented at the Critical Geography Conference, University of Kentucky, Lexington.

Stubbs, J. (2008). Critical criminological research. In T. Anthony & C. Cunneen (Eds.), *The critical criminology companion* (pp. 6–17). Annandale, NSW, Australia: Hawkins Press.

Substance Abuse and Mental Health Services Administration. (2012). *Results from the 2011 National Survey on Drug Use and Health: Summary of national findings* (NSDUH Series H-44, HHS Publication No. (SMA) 12–4713). Rockville, MD: Substance Abuse and Mental Health Services Administration.

Surette, R. (2011). *Media, crime and criminal justice: Images, realities, and policies* (4th ed.). Belmont, CA: Thompson.

Tauri, J.M. (2013). Indigenous critique of authoritarian criminology. In K. Carrington, M. Ball, E. O'Brien, & J.M. Tauri (Eds.), *Crime, justice and social democracy: International perspectives* (pp. 217–233). New York: Palgrave Macmillan.

Taylor, I. (1981). *Law and order: Arguments for socialism*. London: Macmillan.

Taylor, I., Walton, P., & Young, J. (1973). *The new criminology: For a social theory of deviance*. London: Routledge & Kegan Paul.

Thorne-Finch, R. (1992). *Ending the silence: The origins and treatment of male violence against women*. Toronto: University of Toronto Press.

Thoumi, F.E. (2005). The numbers game: Let's all guess the size of the illegal drug industry! *Journal of Drug Issues, 35*, 185–200.

Thurman, K. (1997, July 2). Saga unsettles small-town life. *Christian Science Monitor*, p. 3.

Tigges, L.M., & Fuguitt, G.V. (2003). Commuting: A good job nearby? In David L. Brown and Louis E. Swanson (Eds.), *Challenges for Rural America in the 21st Century* (pp. 166–176). University Park: Pennsylvania State University Press.

Tittle, C.R. (1989). Influences on urbanism: A test of predictions from three perspectives. *Social Problems, 36*, 270–288.

Toews, J.C. (2010, June 10). The disappearing family farm. *Real Truth*. Retrieved May 15, 2012, from http://realtruth.org/articles/100607–006-family.html?print_view=yes.

Tomaszewski, E.A. (1997). "AlterNative" approaches to criminal justice: John Braithwaite's theory of reintegrative shaming revisited. *Critical Criminology, 8*, 105–118.

Tönnies, F. (1955). *Community and society*. Routledge and Kegan Paul.

Toughill, K. (2007, June 9). StatsCan confirms: Small-town folks nicer. *Toronto Star*, p. A1.

Tunnell, K.D. (2004). Cultural constructions of the hillbilly heroin and crime problem. In J. Ferrell, K. Hayward, W. Morrison, & M. Presdee (Eds.), *Cultural criminology unleashed* (pp. 133–142). London: GlassHouse Press.

Tunnell, K.D. (2006). Socially disorganized rural communities. *Crime, Media, Culture, 2*, 332–337.

Turcotte, M. (2005). *Social engagement and civil participation: Are rural and small town populations really at an advantage?* Ottawa: Statistics Canada.

Turk, A.T. (2004). Sociology of terrorism. *Annual Review of Sociology, 30*, 271–286.

U.S. Bureau of the Census. (2010). *2010 urban and rural classification main page*. Retrieved October 11, 2012, from www.census.gov/geo/www/ua/2010urbanruralclass.html.

U.S. Department of Agriculture. (2011). *Rural America at a glance 2011 edition*. Washington, DC: Author.

Useem, J., & Waldner, M. (1942). Patterns of crime in a rural South Dakota county. *Rural Sociology, 6*, 175–185.

Van Dyke, N., & Soule, S.A. (2002). Structural social change and the mobilizing effect of threat: Explaining levels of patriot and militia organizing in the United States. *Social Problems, 49*, 497–520.

Venkatesh, S. (1997). The social organization of gang activity in an urban ghetto. *American Journal of Sociology, 103*, 82–111.

Venkatesh, S. (2000). *American project: The rise and fall of the modern ghetto*. Cambridge, MA: Harvard University Press.

Vieth, V.I. (1998–1999). In my neighbor's house: A proposal to address child abuse in rural America. *Hamline Law Review, 22*, 143–211.

Vold, G.B. (1941). Crime in city and country areas. *Annals of the American Academy of Political and Social Science, 217*, 38–45.

Vold, G.B., Bernard, T.J., Snipes, J.B., & Gerould, A.L. (2009). *Theoretical criminology* (5th ed.). New York: Oxford University Press.

Van Gundy, K. (2006). *Substance abuse in rural and small town America. A Carsey Institute report on rural America*. Durham, NH: Carsey Institute.

Wagner, F., Diaz, D.B., López, A.L., Collado, M.E., & Aldaz, E. (2002). Social cohesion, cultural identity, and drug use in Mexican rural communities. *Substance Use and Misuse, 37*, 715–748.

Walters, R. (2004). Criminology and genetically modified food. *British Journal of Criminology, 44*, 151–167.

Walters, R. (2006). Crime, agriculture and the exploitation of hunger. *British Journal of Criminology, 46*, 26–45.

Wacquant, L. (1997). Three pernicious premises in the study of the American ghetto. *International Journal of Urban and Regional Research, 21*, 341–353.

Ward, O. (2012, December 12). Michigan delivers big blow to unions. *Toronto Star*, pp. A1, A20.

Warner, B.D., & Pierce, G.L. (1993). Reexamining social disorganization theory using calls to the police as a measure of crime. *Criminology, 31*, 493–517.

Warr, M. (2002). *Companions in crime: The social aspects of criminal conduct*. Cambridge, UK: Cambridge University Press.

Waugh, M. (1991). *Smuggling in Devon and Cornwall: 1700–1850*. Newbury, UK: Countryside Books.

Weatherburn, D. (2010). Guest editorial: Indigenous violence. *Australian and New Zealand Journal of Criminology, 43*, 197–198.

Websdale, N. (1995). An ethnographic assessment of policing of domestic violence in rural eastern Kentucky. *Social Justice, 22*, 102–122.

Websdale, N. (1998). *Rural woman battering and the justice system: An ethnography*. Thousand Oaks, CA: Sage.

Websdale, N. (2010). *Familicidal hearts: The emotional styles of 211 killers*. New York: Oxford University Press.

Websdale, N., & Johnson, B. (2005). Reducing woman battering: The role of structural approaches. In N. Sokoloff (Ed.), *Domestic violence at the margins: Readings on race, class, gender, and culture* (pp. 389–415). New Brunswick, NJ: Rutgers University Press.

Webster, J.M., Malteyoke-Scrivner, A., Staton, M., & Leukefeld, C. (2007). Rurality and criminal history as predictors of HIV risk among drug-involved offenders. *Substance Use and Misuse, 42*, 153–160.

Weisheit, R.A. (1992). *Domestic marijuana: A neglected industry*. Westport, CT: Greenwood.

Weisheit, R.A. (1993). Study drugs in rural areas: Notes from the field. *Journal of Research in Crime and Delinquency, 30*, 213–232.

Weisheit, R.A. (2008). Making methamphetamine. *Southern Rural Sociology, 23*, 78–107.

Weisheit, R.A. & Fuller, J. (2004). Methamphetamines in the heartland: A review and initial exploration. *Journal of Crime and Justice, 27*, 131–151.

Weisheit, R.A., Falcone, D.N., & Wells, L.E. (2006). *Crime and policing in rural and small-town America* (3rd ed.). Long Grove, IL: Waveland Press.

Weiss, S. (2002). Review of drinking patterns of rural Arab and Jewish youth in the north of Israel. *Substance Use and Misuse, 37*, 663–687.

Welch, M. (2012). War on terror, human rights, and critical criminology. In W.S. DeKeseredy & M. Dragiewicz (Eds.), *Routledge handbook of critical criminology* (pp. 361–372). London: Routledge.

Wells, L.E., & Weisheit, R.A. (2001). Gang problems in non-metropolitan areas. *Criminal Justice Review, 26*, 170–192.

Wells, L.E., & Weisheit, R.A. (2004). Patterns of rural and urban crime: A county-level comparison. *Criminal Justice Review, 29*, 1–21.

Wells, L.E., & Weisheit, R.A. (2012). Explaining crime in metropolitan and non-metropolitan communities. *International Journal of Rural Criminology, 1*, 154–183.

Welsh, A. (2009). Sex and violence in the slasher horror film: A content analysis of gender differences in the depiction of violence. *Journal of Criminal Justice and Popular Culture, 16*, 1–25.

Welsh, A. (2010). On the perils of living dangerously in the slasher horror film: Gender differences in the association between sexual activity and survival. *Sex Roles, 62*, 762–773.

West, W.G. (1984). *Young offenders and the state: A Canadian perspective on delinquency*. Toronto: Butterworths.

White, R. (2009). Environmental issues and the criminological imagination. In R. White (Ed.), *Environmental crime: A reader* (pp. 62–83). Cullompton, UK: Willan Publishing.

White, R. (2011). *Transnational environmental crime: Toward an eco-global criminology*. London: Routledge.

White, R. (2012). Land theft as rural eco-crime. *International Journal of Rural Criminology, 1*, 203–217.

Whittington, L. (2013, January 8). First Nations eye natural resources. *Toronto Star*, p. A6.

Wiers, P. (1939). Juvenile delinquency in rural Michigan. *Journal of Criminal Law and Criminology, 30*, 211–222.

Wilkinson, K. (1984a). A research note on homicide and rurality. *Social Forces, 63,* 445–452.

Wilkinson, K. (1984b). Rurality and patterns of social disruption. *Rural Sociology, 49,* 23–36.

Wilkinson, K., Reynolds, R.R., Thompson, J.G., & Ostresh, L.M. (1984). Violent crime in the western energy-development region. *Sociological Perspectives, 27,* 241–256.

Wilkinson, K., Thompson, J.G., Reynolds, R.R., & Ostresh, L.M. (1982). Local social disruption and western energy development: A critical review. *Pacific Sociological Review, 25,* 275–296.

Wilkinson, R., & Pickett, K. (2009). *The spirit level: Why equality is better for everyone.* London: Penguin.

Williamson, J.W. (1995). *Hillbillyland: What the movies did to the mountains and what the mountains did to the movies.* Chapel Hill: University of North Carolina Press.

Willits, F.K., & Luloff, A.E. (1995). Urban residents' views of rurality and contacts with places. *Rural Sociology, 60,* 454–466.

Willits, F.K., Bealer, R.C., & Timbers, V.L. (1990). Popular images of "rurality": Data from a Pennsylvania survey. *Rural Sociology, 55,* 449–578.

Wilson, J.M., & Donnermeyer, J.F. (2006). Urbanity, rurality, and adolescent substance use. *Criminal Justice Review, 31,* 337–356.

Wilson, J.Q. (1985). *Thinking about crime.* New York: Vintage.

Wilson, M., & Daly, M. (1992).'Til death do us part. In J. Radford & D.E.H. Russell (Eds.), *Femicide: The politics of women killing* (pp. 83–98). New York: Twayne.

Wirth, L. (1938). Urbanism as a way of life. *American Journal of Sociology, 40,* 1–24.

Wood, D. (1990). *A critique of the urban focus in criminology: The need for a realist view of rural working class crime.* Burnaby, BC: Simon Fraser University, School of Criminology.

Wood, D. (2009). *A review of research on alcohol and drug use, criminal behavior, and the criminal justice system response in American Indian and Alaska Native communities.* Vancouver: Washington State University-Vancouver.

Wood, L.W. (1942). Social organization and crime in small Wisconsin communities. *American Sociological Review, 7,* 40–46.

World Bank. (2013). Rural population (% of total population) in Canada. Retrieved January 8, 2013, from www.tradingeconomics.com/canada/rural-population-wb-data.html.

Young, J. (1975). Working class criminology. In I. Taylor, P. Walton, & J. Young (Eds.), *Critical criminology* (pp. 63–94). London: Routledge & Kegan Paul.

Young, J. (1979). Left idealism, reformism and beyond: From new criminology to Marxism. In B. Fine, R. Kinsey, J. Lea, S. Piccicotto, & J. Young (Eds.), *Capitalism and the rule of law* (pp. 11–28). London: Hutchinson.

Young, J. (1988). Radical criminology in Britain: The emergence of a competing paradigm. *British Journal of Criminology, 28,* 159–183.

Young, J. (1992). Ten points of realism. In J. Young & R. Matthews (Eds.), *Rethinking criminology: The realist debate* (pp. 24–68). London: Sage.

Young, J. (2004). Voodoo criminology and the numbers game. In J. Ferrell, K. Hayward, W. Morrison, & M. Presdee (Eds.), *Cultural criminology unleashed* (pp. 13–28). London: Glasshouse Press.

Young, J. (2007). *The vertigo of late modernity.* London: Sage.

Young, J. (2011). *The criminological imagination.* Malden, MA: Polity Press.

Young, T. (1990). Violent hate groups in rural America. *International Journal of Offender Therapy and Comparative Criminology, 34,* 15–21.

Zeiderman, A. (2006). Ruralizing the city: The great migration and environmental rehabilitation in Baltimore, Maryland. *Identities: Global Studies in Culture and Power, 13,* 209–235.

Zerbisias, A. (2008, January 26). Packaging abuse of women as entertainment for adults: Cruel, degrading scenes "normalized" for generation brought up in dot-com world. *Toronto Star,* p. L3.

Zorza, J. (2002). Domestic violence in rural America. In J. Zorza (Ed.), *Violence against women: Law, prevention, protection, enforcement, treatment, and health* (pp. 14–1–14–2). Kingston, NJ: Civic Research Institute.

INDEX

Page numbers in **bold** denote figures.